# Advance Praise

"When I first encountered Luigi and Dave, I was an aspirational seller who was focused on the wrong tasks and with the wrong mindset—a situation they knew well.

Through their teachings, which are now documented, each theme presented in Sales OS has significantly influenced my sales career, shaping the way I approach every deal and interaction.

Thanks to the insights and strategies shared by the authors, Sales OS encapsulates years of experience into actionable steps that anyone can take immediately.

It's with great admiration and gratitude that I wholeheartedly recommend this invaluable resource to anyone seeking to level up their sales game.

You won't be disappointed!"

—**ALEX CUNNINGHAM**, account director from Evolve AI Labs


"I've known Luigi and David for many years. I've always been impressed by their deep understanding, energy, and passion for solving people's problems with and through sales, delivered in the right way. Their approach to understanding the buyer and meeting their needs resonates with my own experiences.

Sales OS has solid foundations to apply no matter what stage of sales capability you and your teams have in an increasingly digitally disconnected world, with AI looming at us in every direction.

From early days of my tenure at Xero, we've brought Luigi in a few times to upscale and enable our growing ecosystem with sales training. He has been a sought-after speaker we have had back many times across various streams, workshops, and sessions across my career, bringing his energy and passion at every engagement.

Luigi and David are seasoned operators who walk the walk and deploy practical wisdom for all.

Get your pen or highlighter ready because you'll be a better operator from when you first pick up this book to when you put it down.

Best wishes as you continue to invest in your growth, onwards and upwards."

—**BRYAN WILLIAMS**, Founder, Hockey Stick Advisory

"Hey reader, my name is Conor Bell. I've known David and Luigi for nearly five years. If you are reading this, then you've made the excellent choice to up your sales game.

In a world where there are so many sales 'experts,' a book like this is important by showing sales isn't just about selling—it's about building relationships and genuinely trying to help people with problems they are facing.

Sales OS is a framework for helping sellers of all experience levels to put in frameworks to help your customers, and therefore you, to succeed.

Before I knew David and Luigi, I was struggling massively, having gone from a main brand company to a cold sell. The two writers of this book took me under their wing without asking for anything in return. They practice what they preach in trying to help and see it as a relationship.

I'm now at HubSpot at the time of writing this, and I owe the successes I have there to the mentorship that David and Luigi have provided.

When it came to me seeking paid training, you bet it was them I went to first.

If I ever get stuck, you can also bet it's these two who have my back. They are two of the most passionate, knowledgeable, and successful sales professionals I know. But, they are also good people, which makes all the difference when you are trying to find a sales methodology to invest in.

If you are looking for a book by sellers who still sell, who still do the hard yards, who have actionable insight on how to build a successful framework, then this book is for you.

It's more than worthy of your time, and I can guarantee you will learn new ways of thinking. So, don't waste any more time on my view around the two of them; go and read the valuable insights David and Luigi have to share."

—**CONOR BELL**, mid-market growth specialist at HubSpot

"When I first encountered David Fastuca through Entrepreneurs' Organization (EO), I was immediately struck by his drive and dedication. Over the years, I've seen David achieve incredible success, from his time at Locomote to founding Growth Forum with Luigi Prestinenzi, his business partner.

It was a no-brainer for me to collaborate with them to support Ethnolink's growing sales and account management teams.

Ethnolink is Australia's largest translation company. We've grown from a small startup I founded at age 20 in 2011 to a thriving team of 50 full-time team members and 800 contractors.

However, as our business expanded, we faced challenges in consistently ensuring our teams had the best training and support.

This book is significant for anyone in B2B professional services looking to make a bigger impact. When we engaged Growth Forum, we were in a phase of rapid growth. Our sales and account management teams were doing an amazing job figuring things out on their own, but we knew they needed more structured support to continue achieving their targets.

Working with Luigi to systemize our sales processes and provide continuous training and guidance has been transformative for us.

This book encapsulates all the invaluable knowledge that David and Luigi have amassed on B2B sales. It's a must-read for anyone serious about succeeding in this space. The insights and strategies shared in this book are practical, actionable, and rooted in real-world experience.

As you read this book, you'll discover a wealth of knowledge that will help you elevate your B2B sales game. David and Luigi's expertise will guide you through building stronger client relationships and achieving consistent sales success.

Enjoy the journey ahead, and prepare to be transformed by the wisdom within these pages."

—**COSTA VASILI**, Founder and CEO of Ethnolink

"Sales OS offers a much-needed guide for sustainable sales. At a time when integrity is often overlooked, David and Luigi's commitment to transparent, trust-based strategies is essential.

I recall a challenge in my career where adopting principles similar to those in this book helped me achieve success as I continued to build relationships year-on-year despite the previous knock-backs in the FMCG sector.

The fundamental principles of Sales OS—ethical selling, fostering enduring client relationships, and generating predictable revenue—are not just theoretical concepts.

As you delve into the pages of Sales OS, you'll unearth insights that are not just practical, but truly transformative. This book is not merely a guide; it's a powerful manifesto for ethical salesmanship."

—**KATE SAVE**, Co-founder and CEO of Be Fit Food

"As a founder of an outsourcing company specializing in offshore recruitment, my journey in the business world has been one of discovery and continuous learning. As a business owner, I didn't start with any formal sales training.

In the early days, I relied on intuition and the spirit of improvisation. However, as my business grew and I began to build a sales team, I realized the necessity of equipping myself with the knowledge and wisdom from experts in sales.

This book has been a significant resource in that journey.

It offers a framework that deeply resonates with my own experiences and values, particularly the emphasis on truly understanding your customers, focusing on human connection, and building long-term relationships. Sales isn't merely about closing deals; it's about solving real problems and providing genuine value to the other person.

Dave and Luigi bring years of experience in the field and have downloaded their insights into an accessible, easy-to-read format. This is not just another book on sales techniques; it's a little black book based on real-world experience and practical wisdom.

It's a valuable resource for anyone looking to enhance their sales skills, whether you're a seasoned professional or just starting out.

It's been an indispensable tool for me and my team, and I am certain it will be for you as well."

—**LINH PODETTI**, Founder at Outsourcing Angel

"There are a handful of people in life who make a lasting impact, shaping your journey in profound ways. For me, Luigi is at the top of that list. When I first met Luigi, I was comfortable.

Comfortable in my day-to-day routine, complacent about my knowledge, and content with where I was. But Luigi inspired me about what's possible.

Over the years, Luigi has reignited my passion for hard work. He reminded me that it's not just about learning but taking learning to the next level by applying that knowledge, testing it in the real world, and stepping out into a place that's a little uncomfortable.

Thanks to him, I've not only expanded my expertise and driven significant organizational change but also grown as a person. I've become more confident, more curious, and more resilient.

But as much as Luigi has taught me, there's one thing Dave has that Luigi doesn't:

impeccable taste in football clubs. Enter stage left, the often badged "better half" of the duo: Dave.

Dave is driven by values and best practices.

A successful founder and entrepreneur in his own right, his greatest strength is his passion for helping others grow their businesses. As individuals, Luigi and Dave are two of the best practitioners I've had the pleasure of working with.

Together, they are masters of the end-to-end marketing and sales process.

No matter where you are in your marketing or sales career, you can always learn something new from Dave and Luigi.

They have poured their heart, soul, and experience into this book. Sales OS has evolved into a blueprint for success in the modern sales and marketing world.

It encapsulates the wisdom and advice of both Dave and Luigi, as they guide you through the latest research while giving you tested, practical strategies that you can leverage today. It will show you how to think with a growth mindset and see the ever-changing marketing and sales landscape as an opportunity.

As Luigi always tells me, education without application is merely entertainment, so as you read this book, do the work.

Dive in, absorb the knowledge, and let Dave and Luigi show you the way.

I promise, by the end, you'll see the world of sales and marketing through a new lens, and you might just find yourself picking a side in the great Dave vs. Luigi debate."

—**REGAN BARKER**, head of Revenue Operations

"When I first encountered Luigi and David, they were aspirational sales leaders. Over time, they became my mentors and, eventually, my friends.

It would be an understatement to say that we are all struggling with information overload.

Sellers are constantly bombarded with advice from countless self-proclaimed gurus on every possible channel.

What has been desperately missing is a perfectly curated guide that cuts to the core of modern sales.

This book is exactly that.

I've had the privilege of attending David and Luigi's weekly training sessions. Their unwavering belief in the nobility of sales as a profession is inspiring.

They consistently promote ethical selling and emphasize delivering value in every interaction.

To them, selling is about helping others, and they instill this mindset in everyone they train.

The principles in this book have stood the test of time.

They address the fundamental truths of selling while acknowledging how modern buyers prefer to engage. Absorb the knowledge in these pages, put it into practice, and you'll undoubtedly become a top performer.

I encourage you to read this book cover to cover, and then each year, read it again. Its advice will remain as relevant in the future as it is today."

—**RICKY PEARL**, CEO of Pointer Strategy

"I initially met Luigi and Dave when I was a guest expert in the Growth Forum community to run a session on resilience in sales.

Even before the session, I was immersed in the community, blown away by the high-value content and community members. It became one of my most engaged online spaces. Their commitment to their members' growth and success is something for us all to aspire to.

Between being a member of the community, a listener of the podcast, and a fan of the content both Luigi and Dave so generously share on LinkedIn, I've gained valuable insights and strategies that have shifted my approach to sales.

Seeing all this value compiled into the Sales OS gets me fired up.

Not only am I excited to have all their collective knowledge, wisdom, and strategies in one book for my own use, I'm excited for you, the readers who now have access to an MBA in sales at your fingertips.

Get out your highlighters and notebook and see your sales results transform as you implement the 'Sales OS' in your business."

—**STACEY COPAS**, Founder, Academy of Resilience, host of *Resilience Rocks Sales* podcast

"I have known David Fastuca for over a decade, witnessing his remarkable journey in building successful businesses and marketing channels. His dedication and innovative spirit have always impressed me. If only he could apply the same skills to his soccer game, he'd be unstoppable!

This book is an essential read for anyone in sales. It provides a thorough and timely guide, addressing foundational principles and advanced techniques. The focus on developing a growth mindset, understanding deal mechanics, and enabling buyers is particularly relevant in today's dynamic market.

Personally, I have found that adopting a growth mindset and applying strategies similar to those in this book has significantly impacted my own career. The practical advice and actionable insights offered here are invaluable for achieving sales success.

This book goes beyond being a simple guide; it is a comprehensive playbook for ethical and effective salesmanship. Luigi and David's combined experience provides a clear roadmap for navigating the complexities of the sales process.

As you read this book, you will find strategies that are both practical and transformative.

Whether you are a founder or a seasoned sales pro, this book equips you with the tools necessary to excel.

Looking forward to more from you both!"

—**STUART COOK**, founding partner of TWIYO

"Luigi and Dave's fresh perspective on sales in today's world truly resonated with my own professional journey.

This book serves as a must-have guide for B2B sales. In a time when integrity is often overlooked, Luigi and David's unwavering commitment to transparent, trust-based strategies is invaluable.

I remember a time in my career where adopting principles similar to those in this book led to a significant breakthrough. My personal experiences closely align with the insights offered here.

This book is filled with practical strategies you can implement immediately. Luigi and David have distilled years of experience into actionable advice for both seasoned professionals and newcomers."

—**VAL PEREA**, account executive, LinkedIn (a Microsoft company)

LUIGI PRESTINENZI & DAVID FASTUCA

# THE B2B SALES PLAY BOOK

## A TACTICAL GUIDE

### ON HOW TO CREATE A SALES OPERATING SYSTEM THAT CREATES A FLOOD OF QUALIFIED DEALS

**LIONCREST**
PUBLISHING

FIRST EDITION

**THE B2B SALES PLAYBOOK**
*A Tactical Guide on How to Create a Sales Operating System
That Creates a Flood of Qualified Deals*

ISBN  978-1-5445-4647-6  *Hardcover*
      978-1-5445-4646-9  *Paperback*
      978-1-5445-4648-3  *Ebook*

*To our greatest inspiration,*

*Luigi: To Bella and Joey, your curiosity and laughter remind me every day of the importance of connection and passion in everything we do.*

*David: To Chelsea, Leo, and Stella, your energy, bright minds, and loving hearts motivate me to always strive for more, not just in sales but in life.*

*This book is for you.*
*May you always believe in the power of your dreams and the value of sharing your gifts with the world.*

*"Belief is the seed of all possibility.*
*When you believe in something, you set it in motion.*
*When you believe in someone, you lift them*
*higher than they imagined they could go.*
*And when someone believes in you, it becomes*
*the fuel that drives you forward, powering*
*you beyond your own limits."*

—attributed to **NEVILLE GODDARD**

# CONTENTS

Foreword
—Victor Antonio, Sales Velocity Academy ............... xv

Let's Do This Together (Accountability). ................... xvii

Introduction. ............................................. 1

1. The Unseen Foundations of a Sales Journey ............. 11

2. Finding Your Target ................................... 41

3. Deal Mechanics. ...................................... 61

4. Buyer Enablement. .................................... 93

5. Entering the Pursuit ................................. 141

6. Earning the Right ................................... 169

7. Nurturing & Progression ............................. 211

8. The Buying Committee ............................... 239

9. Managing to Close .................................. 259

10. The Power of Human Connection in Sales ............. 287

Conclusion: The Finish Line ........................... 299

Your Voice Matters .................................... 303

Bonus Chapter: Step by Step Playbook to
    Closing an Eight-Figure Deal ....................... 307

About the Authors. .................................... 321

# FOREWORD

## –Victor Antonio, Sales Velocity Academy

The title itself is self-explanatory: The *B2B Sales Playbook: How to Create a Sales Operating System That Creates a Flood of Qualified Deals.* If you're a sales professional, founder, or business leader, the concepts and ideas in this book will help you redefine your sales approach for today's changing market. Luigi and David provide two overarching concepts to structure your sales process.

First, how to implement a V.I.S.I.O.N. Selling Framework to help you or your team build a winning sales mindset by developing a customer-centric approach to selling. It's not about you; it's about how you can best serve your clients.

Second, a Sales OS (Operating System), a system that integrates effective elements of various sales strategies into a cohesive and adaptable framework. It provides a step-by-step guide to help you develop your own sales system, with a focus on:

- Shifting to a growth mindset and embracing the **infinite game** of sales, prioritizing consistent and sustainable actions over cheap, quick wins.
- Defining Ideal Customer Profiles (ICP) and Buyer Personas to target the right buyers.
- Understanding Deal Mechanics, mapping out sales stages and processes to align with the buying process.

- Practicing Buyer Enablement, adding value at each stage of the deal and facilitating a smooth buying journey.
- Building a Sales Plan, defining targets, key accounts, and a cadence for prospecting.
- Mastering cold calling, emailing, and other outreach strategies to effectively connect with prospects.
- Nurturing deals, managing common dynamics, and developing compelling business cases.
- Successfully navigating buying committees, understanding the roles and motivations of different stakeholders.
- Managing objections by recognizing them as requests for more information, addressing concerns, and maintaining progress.
- Closing deals ethically while building long-term relationships.

This is just a sampling of what you'll find in this book, written by two guys who actually sell and who today are closing big deals. If you're struggling to close more deals consistently or you simply want to tap into new markets but don't know how, you'll find plenty of ideas and tactics for rethinking how you sell in the B2B space.

# LET'S DO THIS TOGETHER
## (Accountability)

Welcome! You did it. You got the book.

Now what?

First, the truth: most books don't get read.

They gather dust, stacked with potential energy, reminding you of all the knowledge and outcomes you could have…if only you had the time.

But what if this time was different?

Let us be your accountability partner so you can win more business.

**Register your email over at:** https://growthforum.io/bonuses

We'll dive into a chapter together each week and send you some quick coaching notes to keep you on track and give you end-of-chapter bonuses to help you along your journey.

No fluff, just practitioner-led, actionable insights that'll help you read, absorb, and *actually* apply what you learn.

This could be the only sales guide you ever need if you truly want to roll up your sleeves and do the work.

With a little accountability, you won't just read this book—you'll apply the lessons, frameworks, and strategies.

By the end, you might have a bit of a different idea about what sales is and how to stay healthy and happy while doing it.

# A NOTE FROM THE AUTHORS

In this book, you'll find data and case studies to support the wins we've seen using Sales OS[1] by taking action on the process and principles. To further illustrate key principles, we also share anecdotes from our own business, coaching, and selling experiences, including a powerful interview from one of Luigi's early deals with a large buying committee.

Even though what we aim to present is timeless, as time passes, the context in which a particular approach, strategy, and tactic worked may have changed, or your situation may have important distinctions. Trust your intuition to know the difference and act accordingly.

We believe Sales OS works across industries and in any economic environment *because* we've demonstrated it to work and use it daily ourselves. So have our students, clients, and friends from brands and companies many will recognize.

We like to keep things simple because we are simple people, and we have found that sales, too, is simple. No sense overthinking it. With that, let's go.

---

[1] Sales OS is the program we run over at growthforum.io. It's a Sales Operating System using our V.I.S.I.O.N. Selling Methodology (more on this in the book).

# INTRODUCTION

"I won't get past the first page if it's not engaging with what I want."

—**MARCUS HOOKE**, 17 years at News Corp

## EMBRACING THE CHALLENGE OF SALES

Every interaction with a buyer is unique and happens only once. The first impression, the initial meeting, and the insights that resonate are fleeting yet pivotal moments.

Is the quality of these calls, connections, and conversations random, or is there a way to prepare for greater success?

At Growth Forum, we recognize the impact these singular moments have on the buyer's journey, so we've dedicated ourselves to transforming them from routine checkboxes in a sales funnel into meaningful, value-driven experiences.

In a tough economic landscape dominated by information overload and buyer skepticism, the pressure to find prospects, to have meetings, and to close deals has never been higher. There's a temptation to push harder, and yet many well-worn sales tactics fall flat: instead, buyers align with sellers based on trust and authentic engagement. For example, Marcus Hooke, who provides the interview in this book's Bonus Chapter, says when sellers would reach out to him at News Corp, he would only continue reading their proposal if the first page engaged directly with what he needed.

Once the buyer is engaged, though, any challenges can be overcome with a detailed approach—a system—which gives the buyer everything they need, when they need it.

Luigi embraced these principles to outperform his peers, while David applied Luigi's teaching to build a $150 million pipeline during one of the most challenging economic periods in history.

More to come on that. First, let's introduce you to our overall methodology.

## The V.I.S.I.O.N. Sales Methodology

The core idea in our coaching and in this book is to remove the stigma that surrounds the sales landscape, turning sales into a career of choice, pride, and lifelong craft. To do that, we'd like to introduce the V.I.S.I.O.N. Selling Methodology, which centers on Value, Insights, Strategy, Impact, Outcomes, and Next Steps.

It's a framework that integrates the most effective elements of other sales approaches you may already be familiar with into a cohesive, adaptable system. Far from just closing deals, V.I.S.I.O.N. is a holistic approach aiming to empower sales professionals, founders, and business leaders to think like marketers and become trusted advisors to their clients.

Succeeding with V.I.S.I.O.N. brings unparalleled value at every step, from point A, lining up the first meeting, to point B, helping the Buying Committee reach a confident decision-making point in the buying journey.

## Facilitation Instead of Forcefulness

In today's market, buyers are overwhelmed with information and options. Traditional sales tactics that rely on pressure and persuasion don't work. Can you listen enough to be helpful to those buyers seeking value, authenticity, and genuine partnerships?

The V.I.S.I.O.N. framework addresses this shift by prioritizing the buyer's needs, aligning solutions with their goals, and guiding them through their unique journey with insights and integrity. By doing so, we facilitate successful sales and build relationships based on trust and mutual success.

## Become a Trusted Advisor

The V.I.S.I.O.N. framework empowers you to become a trusted advisor rather than just a seller. By focusing on **Value**, providing deep **Insights**, crafting unique **Strategies**, showcasing real **Impact**, aligning on desired **Outcomes**, and addressing the client's **Next Steps**, you can genuinely assist buyers in seeing new perspectives, overcoming challenges, and achieving their objectives.

You become a trusted advisor through your competence, professionalism, and integrity in the buying journey as the relationship grows.

## What Inspired Us?

Our inspiration stems from witnessing the struggles within the sales industry—complex buyer journeys, extended sales cycles, and a disconnect between sellers and buyers. We saw talented sales professionals feeling overwhelmed by outdated methodologies that didn't align with the modern buyer's expectations and environment.

Recognizing the need for change, we set out to create a system that is both reflective of current market dynamics and adaptable to future shifts.

Stories like Lui outperforming all of his peers combined or David building a $150 million pipeline during COVID-19 highlighted that success isn't just about hard work: it's about working smart with the right approach. These examples fueled our desire to distill what top performers do differently and make it accessible to all.

## The Back Story

In 2012, David co-founded Locomote.com, a SaaS business in the business travel industry—a sector dominated by entrenched, decades-old players. The company faced significant challenges, including moments when it seemed like time and resources had run out. Despite the odds, they successfully exited in 2016, selling for over $30 million to NYSE-listed company Travelport.

In 2021, during the COVID-19 pandemic, a time when the travel industry was crippled, they bought back Locomote for a heavy discount. Recognizing the need for a strong sales strategy in an unprecedented market, David turned to Luigi for sales coaching.

Together, we applied the principles that would later form the foundation of the V.I.S.I.O.N. framework, building a pipeline worth over $150 million in one of the most challenging economic environments.

This experience validated the effectiveness of our approach across different industries and economic conditions. It wasn't just theoretical. It was a proven strategy that delivered tangible results when applied with dedication and effort. Now we're sharing it with you.

## What's Our Philosophy?

At Growth Forum, our philosophy centers around authenticity, continuous learning, and delivering real value. We believe that:

**Sales Is About Relationships:** Genuine connections trump transactional interactions. Building trust based on competence and integrity is paramount.

**Value Over Pressure:** Buyers don't want to be sold to; they want solutions that genuinely address their challenges.

**Systems Drive Success:** A well-designed, adaptable system creates reliability and consistency in results.

**Empowerment Through Knowledge:** By sharing insights and

expertise, we elevate the entire industry and foster a community of growth-minded professionals.

**Sales and Marketing Are Inseparable:** Success comes from integrating these disciplines, thinking like marketers, and selling like trusted advisors.

**Outcome-Oriented Approach:** Success is measured not just in closed deals but in the tangible impact and positive change we facilitate for our clients.

## Join Us on This Journey

The V.I.S.I.O.N. Selling Framework isn't just a new methodology—it's a movement towards a more empathetic, value-driven sales culture. By embracing this approach, sales professionals can navigate the unique challenges of each interaction, provide unparalleled value, and build lasting partnerships that propel both their careers and their clients' businesses forward.

We invite you to join us in redefining sales for the modern era. Whether you're a seasoned salesperson, a founder, or a business leader, the V.I.S.I.O.N. framework offers the tools and insights to elevate your approach and achieve new levels of success.

Together, we can transform the way we connect, communicate, and create value in the world of sales and marketing.

## What Practitioners Will Learn

Now, instead of leaving your success up to the winds of chance or the prevailing economic climate, many are realizing that a sales system is foundational to business survival and growth. Alex Cunningham of Evolve AI Labs said that having a sales system "significantly influenced my sales career, shaping the way I approach every deal and interaction."

What's more, good sales reps are being paid on par with software engineers because good salespeople are one of the best business distribution channels.

Great sales reps can see mid-six-figure compensation. That's because they can more reliably generate business results than, for instance, resources pumped into too many paid ads. (We're not against paid ads; we mix them into our strategy.)

Whether you're a longtime listener of our podcast or a vibrant voice in the Growth Forum community, we're pumped to have you here. You may be a Chelsea fan or an AC Milan fan, but we know you care about sales as a practitioner. Your stories inspire us daily, sharpening the system, tools, and tactics we share.

This book is for those who are selling something every day, whether seasoned or starting a new role.

As practitioners ourselves, we'll touch on the following topics:

- **Chapter 1**: Why your *mindset is the most important attribute* of your sales approach; organizing your mind and tuning it towards learning and growth allows you to first create, maintain, and refine your sales system, which will simplify sales and your life.
- **Chapter 2**: Developing detailed *ideal customer profiles* and *Buyer Personas* to ensure you are targeting the right buyers
- **Chapter 3**: The details of *deal mechanics* so that you can give buyers the information they need at every step to progress confidently to decision
- **Chapter 4**: The finer points of *buyer enablement* in the increasingly complex buyer journey
- **Chapter 5**: How to *enter the pursuit* of buyers, beginning with a sales plan

- **Chapter 6:** What allows you to *earn the right* to talk to prospects
- **Chapter 7:** An exploration of tactics to *nurture and progress deals* at a comfortable pace and rhythm
- **Chapter 8:** The ins and outs of *selling to a buying committee* of any size
- **Chapter 9:** The difference between objections, stalls, and conditions in the latter stages of a deal so that you can *manage to close*
- **Chapter 10:** No matter how many tools become available, *the power of human connection* will always matter in sales because of the lasting outcomes and long-term relationships such connections create.
- **Bonus Chapter:** Laying out *the significant steps in a real deal*, the first eight-figure deal of Luigi's career through an interview with the champion of the Buying Committee

Of course, those are just the main ideas.

If you're someone who only wants the takeaways, the end-of-chapter summary sections and bonuses will serve you well. The templates and resources we've created will put you to work straight away!

> To get access to all of the templates, frameworks, tools, and podcast episodes referenced in this book, visit this link: **growthforum.io/bonuses**

This might be the most interesting time to drive results as a salesperson, so let's get on with it, shall we?

It's time to make how you sell, why you win.

# THE UNSEEN FOUNDATIONS OF A SALES JOURNEY

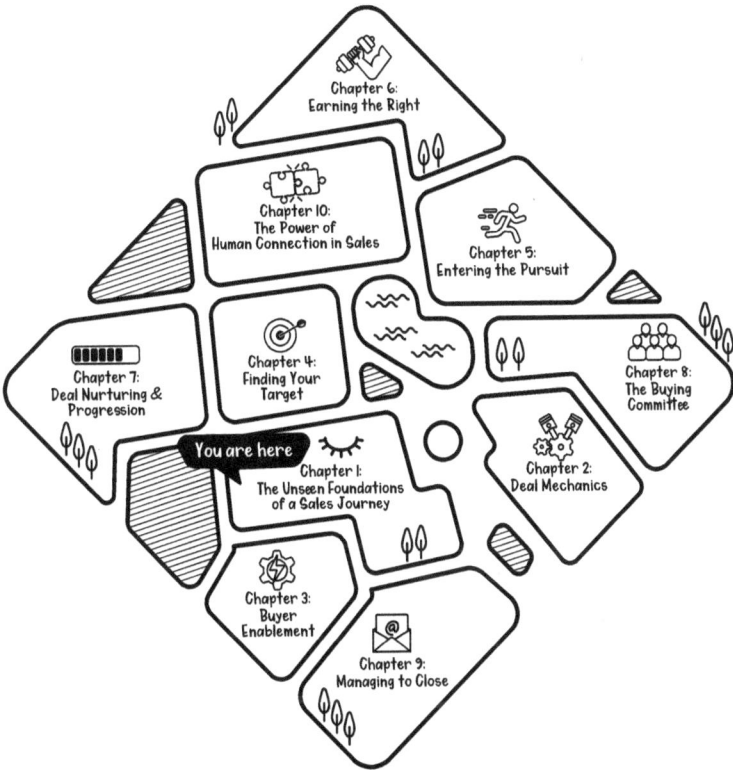

Chapter 6:
Earning the Right

Chapter 10:
The Power of
Human Connection in Sales

Chapter 5:
Entering the Pursuit

Chapter 7:
Deal Nurturing &
Progression

Chapter 4:
Finding Your
Target

Chapter 8:
The Buying
Committee

You are here

Chapter 1:
The Unseen Foundations
of a Sales Journey

Chapter 2:
Deal Mechanics

Chapter 3:
Buyer
Enablement

Chapter 9:
Managing to Close

Why your *mindset is the most important attribute* of your sales approach; organizing your mind and tuning it towards learning and growth allows you to create and intelligently maintain your sales system, which will simplify sales and your life.

Luigi Prestinenzi

Your sales career can only be as good as the mindset you bring to it. No matter your potential, the attitude you approach the work with can separate the good from great salespeople.

Early in my career, I was full of energy but low on formal education. I found myself in telemarketing—a hard job, but one where I picked up invaluable skills by listening closely to what people weren't saying.

It wasn't long, though, before I heard something that would change my life: "You can't sell. Try a different career."

At first, I was angry. How could they not see my potential? But that comment fueled my determination, leading me to commit myself to becoming a lifelong learner and a true sales professional.

Fast forward eight years. I signed that exact company into a $3.5M deal.

Today, I am forever grateful for Loreen's words that I cannot sell. They gave me the intrinsic motivation to be the best version of myself I could be. If I'd quit, I never would have found out where this career has taken me.

Mindset shifts can happen.

The greatest opportunity we have each day is finding a way to get even 0.01% better.

Do this and discover you really do have the will to develop any skill you need in sales.

**One of the ultimate freedoms in life is realizing you have the choice not only of how to react to something that happens, but also, in any situation, however mundane or exciting, in choosing how to think and what to think.**

Although it is hard and takes work, you don't have to accept the automatic or default setting. With practice, you can reach a level of awareness that simply involves paying attention to what is in front of you and what is going on inside of you.

In addition to that core choice, shifting one's mindset to be a sales professional involves:

- Committing to change
- Honing the slight edge on activities that make you valuable
- Controlling what can be controlled

- Integrating coaching (including self-coaching)
- Developing habits that are in line with your goals through careful reflection
- Knowing the importance of perseverance: rejection and NO, a perceived failure, is part of the process

Each of these rounds out the dimensions of (and paths to) a top-performing sales mind. We'll take them one at a time, starting with commitment to change, then close the chapter with a slightly more detailed review of the V.I.S.I.O.N. Sales Methodology.

## COMMITTING TO CHANGE

No book, course, or program can get you to change—not by itself, although it can be a spark and a reminder from your nightstand or bookshelf. There's no change without also applying what is learned. *Doing it* is where the real learning happens. If you pay attention, you can also see yourself changing as you go, which is encouraging. Change is indeed truly part of life experience. Everyone changes. The question is how one will change and at what rate.

For any system to work, including a sales system, it's crucial to look at who is running it.

Without a competent operator—that's you—any system may run less optimally than it might otherwise. But a skilled operator changes the game.

That's why mindset is where this book truly begins. Mindset is in your control. And understanding your mindset will help you to learn and change.

How to change? Or, deeper, how to change one's mind? Practically speaking, change starts by looking in the mirror. Look into your own eyes. Do you like what you see?

If you see room for improvement, you're not alone. Isn't it great that life affords us that chance?

Remember that the status quo bias is perhaps the biggest resistance to change, within you and within any Buying Committee. Learn to recognize it and how to facilitate change.

Understanding the six stages of change will help you reach your short-term goals and long-term objectives. Realizing that such a commitment has its roots in mindset and applies to each stage of the deal and your overall system will help you achieve these goals.

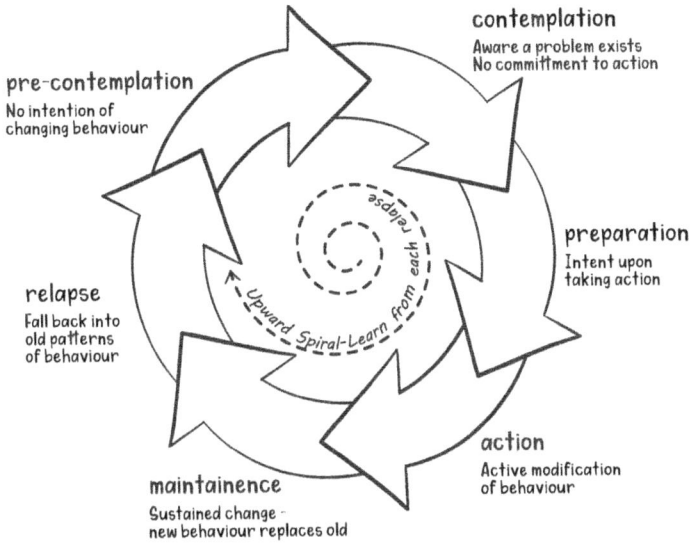

**contemplation**
Aware a problem exists
No commitment to action

**pre-contemplation**
No intention of
changing behaviour

**preparation**
Intent upon
taking action

**relapse**
Fall back into
old patterns
of behaviour

*Upward Spiral-Learn from each relapse*

**action**
Active modification
of behaviour

**maintainence**
Sustained change -
new behaviour replaces old

**Transtheoretical Model of Change**
Prochaska & DiClemente

The principles outlined by Prochaska and DiClemente in their stages of change model provide a compass—the descriptions below give examples from a sales perspective:

1. **Pre-contemplation:** Your initial step is to recognize the need for change. At this stage, the necessity for a shift in approach might not be apparent.
2. **Contemplation:** Here, you begin to acknowledge that enhancing your sales skills requires a change in both behavior and underlying beliefs.
3. **Preparation:** Armed with self-awareness, you identify your strengths and weaknesses, putting your ego aside to critically analyze past experiences and plan for development.
4. **Action:** This is where theory meets practice. You actively engage in new behaviors, honing your skills and adapting your approach to be more customer-centric.
5. **Maintenance:** Sustaining change demands ongoing effort. Regular check-ins, goal setting, and celebrating successes each help to solidify new habits.
6. **Relapse:** Not a failure but a part of the learning process. Relapse offers valuable insights for refinement and growth. It could be that you relapse to solution-selling or other practices that work less well, only to realize again that how you are changing as a seller truly is better for you and for buyers.

It's fine if you're not quite ready to focus only on yourself. The big idea is that change affects everyone, including your buyers and the very systems of which you are a part.

Deciding that part of your *identity* is as a sales professional—it's not *who* you are deep down but a persona you can take on—goes a long way toward adopting and integrating these behaviors, eventually building the habit to where they are second nature through routines that become second nature.

When you act out and explore this persona, you become the facilitator that buyers need you to be.

## Sales First Principles

Imagine hiring a skilled tradesman, such as a carpenter, to undertake a crucial project.

You expect the carpenter to arrive equipped with the necessary tools for the job: a saw, drill, and measuring tape.

As a customer, your confidence in the tradesman's ability is directly linked to their preparedness and professionalism.

Similarly, in the realm of business-to-business (B2B) sales, we are the craftsmen of our trade.

Our tools encompass skills, knowledge, strategies, and a growth-oriented mindset. Self-accountability means taking ownership of our tools. It's about recognizing that our success depends on our readiness to invest in ourselves and leverage the necessary resources.

One goal we stated earlier is to level up the sales profession.

When you decide to be a professional in sales, we believe five principles are necessary because time is limited with buyers who have a more complex buying process than they once did. We can be proactive instead of reactive, relentlessly giving value at the right time, having first listened to and understood our buyers.

These principles guide you to not only meet but exceed customer expectations, fostering long-term relationships and driving success.

1. **Customer-centric approach:** Do you know what your customers value?
2. **Strong communication skills:** Be prepared, be clear, and ask great questions. (Great questions are often simple, well-timed, and well-toned: what motivated you to reach out right now?)
3. **Adaptable and flexible:** Every deal is unique. Pay attention to details and ask, "How am I giving the buyer a great customer experience?"
4. **Persistent and resilient:** Never give up and never compromise on your values, such as honesty and integrity.
5. **Goal-oriented:** 30-60-90-day targets simplify planning and daily actions.

## CONTROL WHAT CAN BE CONTROLLED

Football, some call it soccer—there's no better sport in the world. With literally seconds to go, the result can still be uncertain. And bang. Just like sales. From disaster to success in just one deal.

Forza!

In Italian, the word "forza" means strength or power, and it more subtly means the ability to face the difficulties in life.

We've already discussed how the commitment to embrace change allows for personal and professional growth and the adaptability of your sales operating system.

But what's the most important thing when it comes to mindset? The key to reducing your anxiety and settling into powerful activities is to **control what can be controlled.**

When things are going well, when outcomes are there, that's easy. But can you control what you can control when life pulls you around?

There's a learned wisdom in knowing the difference between things we believe can be controlled (what we wish could be) and those that can actually be controlled by giving them our attention.

Professional athletes know that discipline, practice, and nutrition are all important and under their complete control. The word discipline derives from teaching. Self-discipline is a kind of self-teaching. Practice is repetition and attention to detail. Nutrition to build, restore, and nourish the body. Top athletes decide to stay focused, deliberately practice, and eat the right way. Their consistency in these high-payoff activities is paramount to their success.

Kobe Bryant was known to have practiced every day for multiple hours. In the off-season, he would run, play basketball, and lift weights for a couple of hours each day, six days a week. Alongside Shaquille O'Neal, Kobe led the Los Angeles Lakers to five NBA championships.

Engage the part of yourself that wants *you* to succeed.

In game situations, the storylines may not be going in their favor. But as long as there is still time on the clock, as long as one continues to control what can be controlled, there may come one more chance to turn things around, to snatch success from the jaws of disaster.

Let's also embrace the fact that even when the clock runs out, there is always an opportunity in the next game. You need to be focused and committed to want to win. In *The Greatest Salesman in the World*, Og Magdino wrote: "I will persist until I succeed. I was not delivered unto this world in defeat, nor does failure course in my veins. I am not a sheep waiting to be prodded by my shepherd. I am a lion, and I refuse to talk, to walk, to sleep with the sheep."

## The Slight Edge Mentality

Building on the activities that can be controlled, is there a way to zoom in on those skills that make the most difference?

In professional golf, on the PGA Tour in 2023, less than two strokes (68.3 versus 70.1) per 18 holes separated the #1 and #30 golfers in the world, but that difference meant a gap in total earnings of $15.5 million ($21M versus $5.5M). That nearly same two-stroke difference (67.9 versus 69.8) in performance so far in 2024 between #1 and #30 has led to an even larger pay gap of $24M ($28M versus $4M).

In golf, the short game is crucial. Whether approach shots, pitches from the rough around the green, or getting up and down out of the sandy bunkers, all these require various specific skills that must be practiced. Because the game of golf occurs not on a flat surface but in a fractal environment, no shot is the same as another. (Just as no sales interaction is exactly like another.)

Golf is not *all* short game though. If you can drive it long enough to reach greens on a par 4, then right away you're putting for eagle, when others still have to chip on first to putt for birdie at best. (Having a humming sales system is like having a great long game in golf. The short game is executing on all the finer details.)

*These days, good sales reps are often being paid on par with software engineers because good salespeople are one of the best business distribution channels.*

It is worth figuring out where you, as a salesperson, have a slight edge that makes a big difference and then maintaining that edge. For some, it is knowing their target audience extremely well so they can immediately connect energetically with anyone in that group. For others, it is the overall efficiency of their system to reliably provide quality leads.

### Training Without Application Is Simply Entertainment

One of the best parts of coaching is witnessing others achieve awesome outcomes.

While coaching high performers from great companies like Stripe, HubSpot, and DocuSign, we noticed this: they all take action.

So, as much as we would like to take credit as coaches, we can't.

A practice that goes along with simply taking action and sets apart those who achieve better-than-average outcomes or even top 1% results is this: beginning to apply what one has learned *soon after learning it*. Think of this as spaced repetition augmented by experiential learning.

While many of you will read this chapter, those who find ways to apply it when you put the book down—or better, put the book down now to apply one thing you've learned—will have a greater chance of improving as sales professionals over the long run.

One of the salespeople we've enjoyed working with is Val Perea. Her growth has come from setting aside fear and going for it. She changed careers and became a top 1% salesperson for LinkedIn.

What we love about sales is that anything is possible. You don't need a degree. All you need is the will to develop the skill.

### Coaching as a Strategy for Improvement

B2B sales is not everyone's cup of tea—it's highly competitive, and only those who can overcome failures can succeed.

So what can we do to improve and eliminate these setbacks?

In our professional lives, coaching is often synonymous with external guidance from managers, team leaders, or specialized coaches within our organizations.

We look to these individuals for insights, feedback, and strategies to enhance our sales performance.

External coaching undoubtedly plays a crucial role in our growth by providing valuable perspectives and expertise.

It's a great tool. We gain new perspectives and learn new methods to avoid failed calls.

Plus, coaching seems to be effective and popular. Recent statistics show this niche has a $5.34 billion market share, and the figures are only expected to grow.

However, coaching is not solely an external endeavor. It's also a strategy for continuous improvement that can be amplified through self-coaching.

**Imagine if we could harness the power of coaching from within ourselves instead of just from others.**

Self-coaching empowers us to take charge of our development journey, becoming active participants in our own growth.

# When I Chose to Demote Myself

My career took a major leap when I chose to demote myself.

I was running our business-to-business sales team.

Hitting targets, I was in my comfort zone.

Yet I noticed a gap in my abilities, particularly in managing the consumer sales funnel.

So I made the choice to step down, placing myself under the guidance of a colleague.

This decision radically transformed my career.

It allowed me to fill in the gaps in my knowledge. Elevating my career to heights I hadn't imagined.

Often, the key to advancing forward is knowing when to step back.

And checking your ego at the door.

I am forever grateful to you, Craig Holmes. You're one of the best leaders I have had the privilege to work with and learn from.

Healthy humility is often the first step to learning.

## Becoming Your Own Self-Coach

What is self-coaching? Self-coaching allows us to take ownership of our growth and refine our skills autonomously.

You may think of it as a way of telling yourself what to do, but it's not. Doing that, you'd probably just place undue pressure on yourself and start feeling negative emotions.

Instead, we can look at it this way—self-coaching is about introspection and reflection at every stage of the sales process. It's about carving out intentional time to assess our interactions with clients and prospects.

When was the last time you asked yourself, "What aspects of my approach worked well in that recent sales call? What could I have done differently to enhance the outcome?"

By posing these two simple yet profound questions to ourselves, we open the door to new insights and perspectives.

## Great Coaching Doesn't Tell You What You Should Have Done

There's a difference between a proactive and reactive mindset.

Choose to be proactive.

We can't control whether we receive coaching from someone else. But we can evaluate our previous calls and processes.

Therefore, effective coaching isn't about receiving answers or directives. It's about being asked (and asking ourselves) the right questions that challenge us to think differently and grow.

Face-to-face coaching sessions can be less accessible due to hybrid work setups and remote interactions.

This is where self-coaching emerges as a valuable strategy.

By embracing self-coaching, we become the architects of our development journey.

We cultivate self-awareness, identify areas for improvement, and implement actionable changes independently.

## Learning Through Rejection

Rejection hurts. Nobody likes it. But it doesn't have to be a bad thing. Here's why:

- Rejection is proof you're taking action.
- Rejection is an opportunity to learn and improve.
- Rejection brings you closer to a "yes."
- Rejection makes the wins even sweeter.

The best way to deal with rejection is to embrace it.

- Make it a game.
- Make it a challenge.
- Make it a part of your sales process.

Don't avoid it. Don't fear it.

Embrace it. Instead of feeling helpless, let it help you grow.

## Checkpoint 1:
## Mindset

*Just as there are checkpoints in a sales and buying journey, there will be checkpoints through this book to test your learning and application: learning without application is simply entertainment.*

### Self-Coaching Audit

*What kind of self-coach are you? Do you practice what your self-coach preaches? Think of one example where you've followed your own encouragement and one example where you missed the mark. How will you alert yourself to ensure you speak up, take the right action, or hit the target next time?*

## REFLECTION IN THE CONTEXT OF B2B SALES

In our quest for continuous improvement in B2B sales, one of the most impactful strategies we can adopt is intentional reflection.

### 1. Ask the Right Questions

After each client interaction or sales call, take a moment to pause and reflect.

Ask yourself two pivotal questions I mentioned above:

- What did I do right during this interaction?
- What could I have done differently to potentially change the outcome?

It's essential to avoid fixating solely on the negatives.

Instead, focus on celebrating your strengths and pinpointing areas for refinement.

By adopting this reflective mindset, you cultivate self-awareness and pave the way for meaningful growth.

My tip when self-reflecting is to do it for 10 to 15 minutes after a call. This process will serve as a debriefing of sorts.

Reflection helps you slow down your brain and get ready for the next call. It releases tension and helps temper your mood so you can become the person that prospects want to talk to.

Nobody wants to engage with a stressed or moody person, right?

## 2. Documenting Your Insights:
## The Power of Daily Reflection

Capture your reflections by writing down your answers to these questions in a daily journal or digital notebook.

Documenting your insights in real time ensures that valuable lessons are captured and retained. Over time, this journal becomes a treasure trove of actionable insights that can inform your sales strategies.

## 3. Leveraging AI for Deeper Analysis

Artificial intelligence (AI) is here to stay, and we should embrace it as a tool to help with our self-coaching pursuits because they can sift through vast amounts of data efficiently.

At the end of the week, revisit your journal notes and leverage the power of AI tools to identify patterns and trends as well as to highlight recurring themes or areas that require attention, whether in sales performance or customer interactions.

## 4. Transforming Insights into Strategies

Armed with these insights, you should take proactive steps to refine your approach for future sales calls.

Identify recurring challenges or opportunities for improvement and devise tailored strategies. For instance, if you notice a pattern of successful engagements stemming from personalized follow-ups, leverage this insight to enhance your outreach tactics.

Making these changes regularly will align you more quickly with your goals.

# Knowing When to Get a Coach

David Fastuca

**DAVE HERE:** it's okay if you don't want to rely only on yourself.

I started out in business at age 14, selling my graphic design services to anyone who was interested, whether door-knocking or cold calling. It's been fun to see our students succeed in Growth Forum, as well as watching Luigi refine his approach as a practitioner and even develop new buyer enablement concepts with P3 Recovery, where the deal cycles are wrapping up in under 30 days, where that market usually takes 90–120 days minimum, as will be discussed in Chapter 3: Buyer Enablement.

Luigi coached me on the sales process that we are going to teach you in this book, the same one we have taught to those in our Sales OS (Operating System) course online at GrowthForum.io.

It's the process that helped me build a $150M+ pipeline for a business travel company during COVID-19. Let that sink in.

That was for a company called Locomote, which I started with my cousin (Ross) in 2012, when I was 26. We exited in 2016, selling for $30M+, then bought it back for a heavy discount during COVID-19 and built it up again. I then decided my time in the travel industry was done, and it was time to focus on my real passion, helping those in sales and marketing achieve their goals, so in March 2023, I left Locomote to start Growth Forum with Luigi and haven't looked back.

The number of times I have to step in on his deals to move things along makes me wonder if he learned anything from my coaching...

## THE SELLER SCORECARD

The journey to sales success is paved with daily discipline and creativity and play. (Yes, play. Notice the top tennis pros play with their racket between points to temporarily lower the seriousness of what they are doing.)

Embrace habits that foster learning, prospecting, creating content, and networking. Time-block critical tasks and remain laser-focused on activities that drive pipeline progression. Avoid the allure of quick fixes and remain committed to the fundamentals, understanding that true excellence comes from mastering the basics.

Craig Ballantyne, strength and conditioning coach and author of *The Perfect Day Formula*, said, "Everything you do either sets you up for success or puts another obstacle in the way."[2]

Consider these additional tips, too:

- Architect the day so you are in control, not others
- Time-block tasks in the calendar so no one can book time in over it, ensuring there is time to get the work done
- Plan the night before, and the week before each Friday

You might think that top-performing athletes are in a league of their own when it comes to their activities. But actually, even though their performance seems superhuman, what they do to get there is not.

What they do have is discipline in activities that set them apart.

You and I can follow these same general practices to improve as salespeople—to truly become a sales professional—and be well on your way to the top 1% in your company.

Go ahead and fill out this scorecard right now.

Seller Scorecard: Rate Yourself Like a Top Performing Athlete

- How much of your pipeline is self-sourced? (6 points)
- Do you time-block every week to prospect? (5 points)
- Do you prepare before a discovery call? (5 points)
- Do you use a pre-call planner? (5 points)
- Do you multi-thread before or after a meeting? (4 points)
- Do you use mutual action plans? (4 points)

---

[2] "Craig Ballantyn: Get Out There and Do," interview by Luigi Prestinezi, January 26, 2022, in *How to Sell: B2B Founder Growth Systems*, podcast, 36:06, https://open.spotify .com/episode/330hp2lMtLfCILjTDr5Xyh?si=TwwvreDiRsGUfau6Z18UXA&nd=1&dlsi =9f484f8de28f40d1.

- Do you send your meeting notes post-meeting? (5 points)
- Discovery questions? (5 points)
- Do you send your proposal or present it first? (5 points)
- How confident are you in writing a business case? (6 points)

How many points did you get out of 50?

- Less than 42? Let's up your game! (Choose one area to improve right now.)
- More than 42 but less than 50? Doing well, but room to grow. (Improve one area.)
- 50/50? Pick one of these activities and audit yourself, asking:
  - → What am I doing well but could become world-class at?
  - → What's my weakest attribute that's limiting my growth?

## Seller Scorecard: Rate Yourself Like a Top-Performing Athlete

| Questions: Score yourself out of 5 (With 5 being highest and 0 being lowest) | Example | You |
|---|---|---|
| How much of your pipeline is self-sourced? | 3 | |
| Do you time block every week to prospect? | 3 | |
| Do you prepare before a discovery call? | 4 | |
| Do you use a pre-call planner? | 3 | |
| Do you multi-thread before or after a meeting? | 5 | |
| Do you use mutual action plans? | 4 | |
| Do you send your meeting notes post meeting? | 5 | |
| Discovery questions? | 3 | |
| Do you send your proposal or present it first? | 4 | |
| How confident are you in writing a business case? | 4 | |
| **Total** | 38 | |

## How many points did you get out of 50?

Less than 42? Let's up your game!

More than 42 but less than 50? Doing well, but room to grow.

50/50? Pick one of these activities and audit yourself, asking:
1) What am I doing well but could become world-class at?
2) What's my weakest attribute that's limiting my growth?

# THE V.I.S.I.O.N. SALES METHODOLOGY

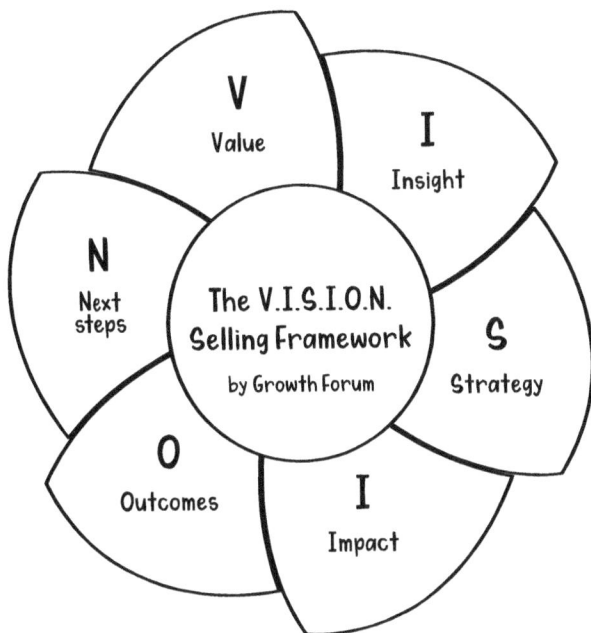

Now that we've talked a bit about improving your mindset and why mindset is essential to a successful sales career, let's apply that winning mindset to a deeper look at the V.I.S.I.O.N. Sales Methodology to further help you understand our sales worldview.

What is the essence of the methodology, and why did we create it?

A lot of sales philosophies and processes talk purely about the sales process. Then there's marketing, which, like sales, addresses both processes and people. Fundamentally, though, sales and marketing will both serve that buyer through the buyer journey.

In a recent multibillion-dollar company that we've just won, there were about 13 people that we had to bring to decision. The complexities and the bureaucracy connected for these big accounts is significant.

V.I.S.I.O.N. is about facilitating buyers through the decision-making journey and guiding to avoid No Decision, the enemy. What often leads to No Decision is the status quo bias. It kicks in to stop a deal even if the benefits are clear.

Connecting the current and future state to overcome the status quo is also key to V.I.S.I.O.N. Allow the Buying Committing to see that path. Where are they today, and how do they get where they want to go tomorrow?

## Value

In this context, value is about guiding buyers to see a new perspective. Their challenges and opportunities can be seen from 40,000 feet up.

What value is not: the product you offer, the features, the ROI. Instead, it's foremost the different overview you've offered that begins the buying and selling process.

## Insight

Once the buyer is seeing the challenge from a new perspective, what are the alternatives?

How are others approaching this? Evaluation can then happen.

## Strategy

Buyers don't often have a clear pathway forward. That's why we have to help them create a strategy. What does that roadmap look like and who is involved? How does the past influence their decision-making today?

Build a clear strategy on how to get from Point A to Point B.

The business case will drive the strategy.

## Impact

This is about the *change*.

There's going to be some form of discomfort or pain that goes along with change. Businesses will do multiple risk assessments before buying anything.

Be transparent about the challenges because this is what a trusted advisor does. Being a consultant doesn't mean painting a rosy picture. Instead, clarify the business case through an evaluation of what could work and what could go wrong.

## Next Steps

Progress doesn't happen by chance—it happens by design. At Growth Forum, we understand that clearly defined next steps are crucial for maintaining momentum and driving deals forward.

By collaboratively outlining a roadmap with your prospect, you ensure that both parties are aligned and committed to the journey ahead. (It's possible to remind buyers of the cost of inaction here as well.) This proactive approach keeps the engagement active, minimizes uncertainties, and accelerates the decision-making process.

By focusing on actionable next steps, you not only demonstrate your dedication to their success but also make it simpler for your prospect to move forward with confidence.

## SOUND BYTE SUMMARY

—  Salespeople are judged on performance, and your mindset is your number one contributor to your short- and long-term success.

—  A learning mindset makes you coachable (and self-coachable), allowing you to learn and apply what you've learned immediately and through spaced repetition.

— Becoming a sales professional is sometimes as simple as declaring, "I am a sales professional." The choices and behaviors, such as authentic communication and lifelong learning, will flow from that statement.

— Treat rejection as a chance to learn and a reminder that you are taking action in the infinite game of sales.

— Embrace the V.I.S.I.O.N. Sales Methodology for a holistic approach to helping buyers along the buying journey, filling information gaps at every step.

To get access to all of the templates, frameworks, tools, and podcast episodes referenced in this book, visit this link: **growthforum.io/bonuses**

## NEXT UP...

Before we dive into actually building out your sales process, it's necessary to lay the right foundation—so *who* are you actually selling to?

# FINDING YOUR TARGET

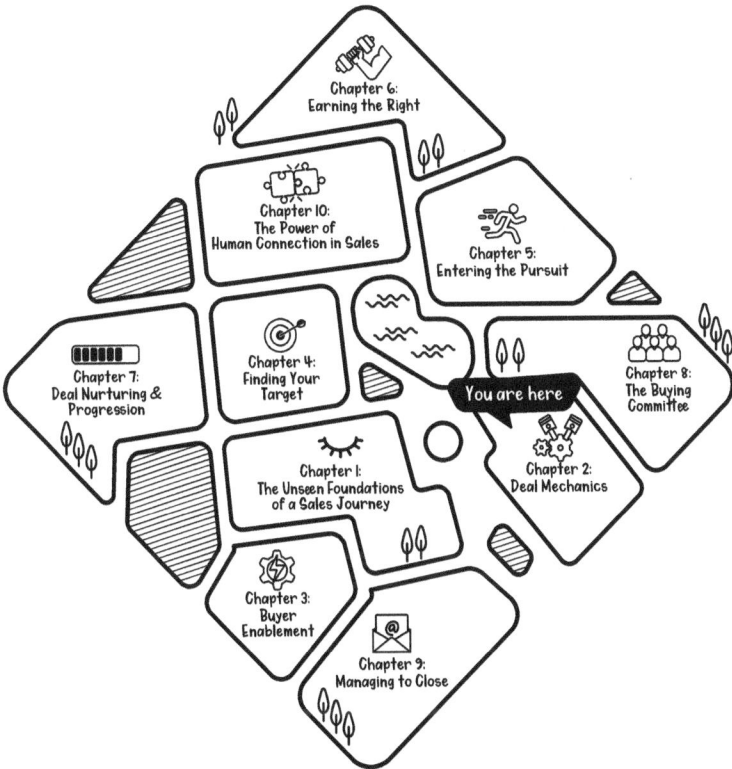

Chapter 6:
Earning the Right

Chapter 10:
The Power of
Human Connection in Sales

Chapter 5:
Entering the Pursuit

Chapter 7:
Deal Nurturing &
Progression

Chapter 4:
Finding Your
Target

You are here

Chapter 8:
The Buying
Committee

Chapter 1:
The Unseen Foundations
of a Sales Journey

Chapter 2:
Deal Mechanics

Chapter 3:
Buyer
Enablement

Chapter 9:
Managing to Close

# Developing detailed *Ideal Customer Profiles* and *Buyer Personas* to ensure you are targeting the right buyers

A re you wasting time chasing leads that will never close? In sales, the difference between winning and losing often comes down to one thing: targeting the right buyer from the start.

In the high-stakes world of sales, where the clock is always ticking, focusing your energy on the right buyers isn't just strategic—it's crucial.

Many salespeople start hitting accounts before they've truly thought about who to target. We've heard "We're targeting a variety of businesses." But one early guest on our podcast questioned whether everyone is truly our customer.

We can't develop our sales process (which you'll start in the next chapter) without first defining exactly who we are targeting. The acquisition strategy comes after that first puzzle piece is set.

You might be thinking, *But what I really need to know is who I am and what I represent in order to figure out who I should be targeting.*

That's true. You certainly need to know yourself (mindset) and be up to speed on the landscape in which you're operating, especially when starting in a new role. *Know your offer.* (But you will of course not be *leading* with your offer.) Only then are you ready to figure out who you should be talking to.

And that's where the Ideal Customer Profile (ICP) and Buyer Persona come in. These tools and exercises let us practice getting granular with all the details around *the people*—your buyers—that we'll be interacting with throughout the buying journey.

What comes after that, in Chapter 3: Deal Mechanics, is laying out each stage in the deal so that we know what to give our buyers at each stage, exactly what they need, exactly when they need it, to eventually progress to a confident point of decision.

You need to earn the right to enter the pursuit with a prospect. Over 80% of buyers want a salesperson-free interaction. Why? Because many salespeople show up unprepared.

Engaging in the wrong activities, accounts, or prospects doesn't just eat up your day; it directly harms your pipeline and, ultimately, your ability to meet or exceed your sales target. In a field where performance is not just observed but measured and judged, understanding where to direct your efforts can mean the difference between growth and being stagnant.

According to SaaStr, the average tenure of a sales development rep hovers around 14 months, a timeframe highlighting the intense pressure to perform. Amidst this, the allure of tech and automation can sometimes lead to inefficient practices, such as bloating the top of the funnel with quantity over quality, thus diluting the very essence of effective salesmanship.

In recent years, the percentage of time that salespeople actually spend selling has decreased to less than a third of their working time, the rest being taken up by admin, data entry, tool management, and other tasks that just aren't selling.

But even if we do spend more time selling, we could be selling to the wrong people...

When we met Conor, even though he is a big Liverpool fan, we still decided to work with him and help him (haha)! He had just made a big move to HubSpot and wanted to get off on the right foot.

His focus when he started was small to medium businesses (SMB). However, what he was failing to do was define that market into categories or segments. As a result, his message struggled to connect with the target audience.

So we started by getting very clear on who within the SMB space he should be targeting.

Then, he focused on particular segments within that SMB market. His messaging was tailored, and it started resonating with the audience—his list-building became a lot clearer, too.

Speaking to a qualified list with the value they wanted had a domino effect through his pipeline, bolstering his deal outcomes.

Spending too much time on the wrong accounts can cause unneeded stress trying to make quota, but Conor refocused on the people who were a better fit for him by honing his ICP, which carried him all the way to President's Club.

## THE IDEAL CUSTOMER PROFILE

The ICP is the base of your prospecting campaign, but let's be specific about why we should use it.

**When we develop our ICP, it's the first step in getting our foundations right that allows us to later develop our full sales process.**

As sales professionals, we don't have unlimited time to prospect. In fact, according to HubSpot, as much as 50% of salespeople's pipelines are filled with the wrong type of opportunities. Allowing the wrong deals to crowd our schedules violates the Pareto Principle, where a small percentage of key activities (and accounts) garner the lion's share of impact.

Why spend so much time on opportunities that might never close? Identifying these takes a bit of work and sober reflection. If a salesperson *knew* in advance the likelihood of certain opportunities ever closing being near zero, would they even pursue them? Likely not. With experience we can level with ourselves and rule certain opportunities out very early on.

Let's unpack this. Even if some of the wrong opportunities do close, if they aren't the right fit for what you sell, those customers could become problematic and then churn out or even request a full refund, putting you in the negative.

With an ICP built out, you'll be able to filter your searches, refine your searches, and build effective targeting lists to make it easier for you to prospect.

To confirm your ICP, it's essential to avoid the wide net of Total Addressable Market (TAM) and instead zoom into the more relevant segments of Serviceable Addressable Market (SAM) and Serviceable Obtainable Market (SOM).

Why? Because the TAM can sometimes be deceiving. We look at the entire addressable market and think, WOW, look at how much potential business I can win! But the TAM is not our target.

Here's a simple example: Let's say you sell software for small businesses. Your **TAM** could include every small business in the country, but realistically, your **SAM** might be businesses that use a certain kind of technology. Your **SOM** narrows it even further to those actively looking for solutions like yours.

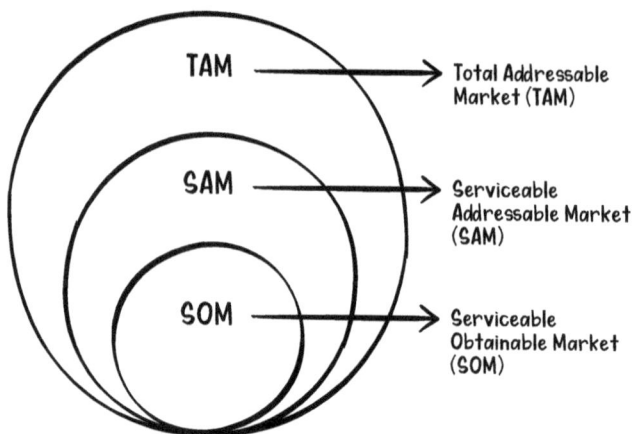

As the great man Seth Godin says, "Everyone is not your customer."

This focus not only streamlines your efforts but also enhances the precision and impact of your sales activities. Building a Buyer Persona further refines this process, adding layers of depth and detail to your understanding of who you're selling to, thus making your outreach efforts more personalized and effective.

The ICP is an incredible tool to help you build and refine your searches. But those searches will be way off if you don't filter based on certain attributes.

So what are the elements of building an ICP?

- Firmographics, also known as corporate demographics
- Direct and Indirect Influencers
- What They Focus On
- Goals, Objectives, KPIs
- Challenges and Frustrations
- Objections Anticipated
- Words that Connect
- Trigger Events

## Director of Sales

### What They Focus On

| | |
|---|---|
| Coaching | Managing pipeline and delivering reports on performance |
| Engaging the team to keep them motivated | Attending sales calls |
| Interviewing new hires and help with onboarding | Managing exec expectations |

### Demographics

| | |
|---|---|
| Age | : 35 to 55 |
| Education | : Bachelor's or Master's |
| Average Tenure | : 5 Years |
| Reports To | : CEO |
| Buyer Type | : – Decision Maker<br>– Economic Buyer |

### Goals | Objectives | KPIs

| | |
|---|---|
| Quota Attainment | Forecast Accuracy |
| Pipeline Coverage x 4 | Meeting Growth and Acquisition Targets |
| Cost Per Acquisition under 20% | Retention and Growth |

### Direct Influencers

CEO

Sales Team

Enablement Team

Customer Success

### Challenges and Frustrations

| | |
|---|---|
| Time Poor | Pressure from the CEO to deliver on strong growth targets |
| Sales team not prospecting enough opps | Marketing not delivering enough qualified leads |
| Not enough pipeline | Deals not being managed properly and CRM not being updated |
| Win rates not high enough | 65% of sales team not hitting target |

### Indirect Influencers

Friends

Customers

Uni Alumni

Linkedin Groups

### Objections to Anticipate

We are too busy to consider anything new

We already have a CRM

No budget

### Words that Connect

More reps hitting target

Increase Forecast Accuracy

Shorter sales cycle

### Trigger Events

Capital Raise

New Hires

Acquisition

In constructing these, you can also allow a little automation to assist you. Below is a template you can use. Start by heading over to your favorite generative pre-training transformer (GPT), such as ChatGPT.

By leveraging AI tools like ChatGPT or Claude, you can streamline the process of building your ICP and Buyer Personas. Instead of starting from scratch, use AI to generate a strong first draft, which you can then refine based on your unique insights.

# Prompt for Ideal Customer Profiles

We wanted to cover not just your run-of-the-mill demographics and pain points but also psychographics and opportunities.

This allows us to get to know our prospects more and leverage them for personalization—which is really useful if you're using methods such as account-based marketing (ABM) in your marketing strategy.

**Here's what it looks like:**

I'm a *what do you do for a living* who is selling a *product/service* that *what does it do*.

Here are other details of the service:

- *detail about the product/service*
- *detail about the product/service*
- *detail about the product/service*

My USP is *what is your USP*. My *product/service* starts at *pricing*.

I need to create *number* comprehensive ideal customer profiles. Be very specific about the details you provide.

These should include the following:

- Job and industry information
- Demographics
- Psychographics
- Challenges and pain points
- Goals and aspirations
- Technological proficiencies
- Opportunities
- Content I should use to reach them
- Channels they're on

The prompt starts with some context on yourself to show ChatGPT (or whatever is your AI tool of choice) what you specialize in.

We then move on to the context of the product or service you're selling. You want to give it a quick executive summary and then work your way into three—or more—highly specific details of what you offer.

Be detailed with these points.

Next, include your USP (unique selling proposition) and your sample pricing. This helps ChatGPT eliminate particular profiles that might not be able to afford your services. We added this part to give you some form of lead qualification right off the bat.

Now, once you're done filling all of this out, double-check what you have and hit that enter button!

By completing the ICP, you'll be part of the way through to completing the Buyer Persona as well.

## BUYER PERSONA

To complement the ICP, build out your Buyer Personas.

With it, you'll have a clear understanding of who you are speaking with—for every member of the Buying Committee, which could be large!—and how to add value to every conversation.

We'll go into much more detail on this in upcoming chapters, but if Buying Committees are of a certain size, start with the champion and key economic decision-makers, then expand as you learn who all the players are in that decision.

Remember, leaving out any key decision-maker could mean a surprise objection unnecessarily slows down the deal.

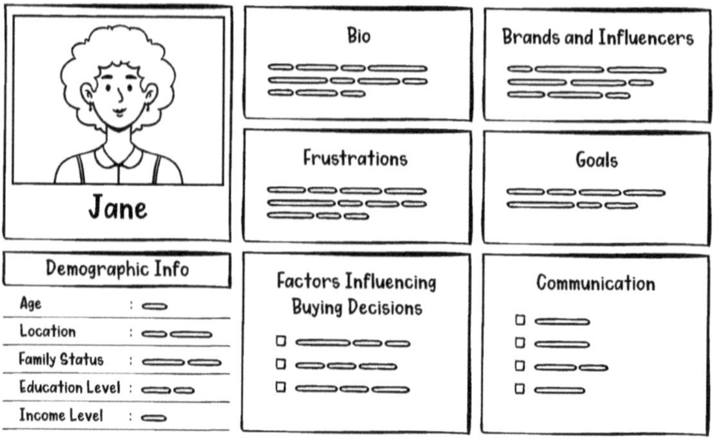

The following is a persona card layout with these sections:

| Jane | Bio | Brands and Influencers |
| --- | --- | --- |
| | Frustrations | Goals |

| Demographic Info | Factors Influencing Buying Decisions | Communication |
| --- | --- | --- |
| Age : | | |
| Location : | | |
| Family Status : | | |
| Education Level : | | |
| Income Level : | | |

There are a number of ways to build out the Buyer Persona(s), including using an AI cheat code as was done above with the ICP. If you know what you're doing, it doesn't hurt to design with a bit of automation.

## Step 1: Basics

Ask to generate your persona's demographic and psychographic profile.

"Generate a basic demographic and psychographic profile for a typical buyer persona interested in [product/service]."

## Step 2: Goals and Challenges

Request possible goals and challenges your persona might encounter. What are they trying to achieve? What obstacles are in their way?

"What could be the typical goals and challenges of a buyer persona using [product/service]?"

### Step 3: Values and Fears

Ask for potential values and fears your persona might have.

"What values and fears might a buyer persona have when considering [product/service]?"

### Step 4: Information Sources

Determine which information sources your persona might trust.

"What sources of information might a buyer persona trust when researching [product/service]?"

### Step 5: Customer Journey

Define your persona's thought process from identifying a need to making a decision.

"Describe the customer journey for a buyer persona from realizing a need to making a decision about [product/service]."

### Bonus

Feel free to ask any other questions you might have about the Buyer Persona's habits, preferences, or behaviors.

"What could be the primary reasons for [buyer persona] to switch to our competitors?"

"How might [buyer persona] react to a price increase in our product/service?"

"Which social media platforms does [buyer persona] most likely use?"

"What kind of customer support might [buyer persona] expect from us?"

"How can we turn [buyer persona] into a loyal, long-term customer?"

**But wait, there's more! We have three hacks up to help you make the most out of ChatGPT.**

### Reducing Errors

For a detailed answer, break down any response into step-by-step instructions. Use this prompt:

"Let's work this out in a step-by-step way to be sure we have the right answer."

### The Self-Check

Make ChatGPT check its previous answers for flaws and weak arguments with this prompt:

"You are a researcher tasked with investigating the [previous answer] response options provided. List the flaws and faulty logic of each answer option. Let's work this out in a step-by-step way to be sure we have all the errors."

### The Resolver Strategy

Use this prompt to create a comprehensive response:

"You are a resolver tasked with (1) finding which of the [previous] answer options the researcher thought was best, (2) improving that answer, and (3) printing the improved answer in full. Let's work this out in a step-by-step way to be sure we have the right answer."

Completing Buyer Personas makes you truly pause and think about which buyers you are serving and how you might help them.

Know who you are talking to and what they care about so that communication is easier and adds value. End-users, executive sponsors, economic decision-makers, each will have a different role within the Buying Committee.

Remember: an ICP helps you define the types of companies you should target—those most likely to benefit from your product. With a Buyer Persona, on the other hand, we zoom in on the specific individuals within those companies who will make the buying decisions.

Next, you'll be able to craft messages that resonate with each of these buyers.

Finally, having understood the psychology within the Buyer Personas, you can map customer journeys and persona-specific value propositions. (All this is coming up in Chapter 6: Earning the Right.)

## Checkpoint 2:
## Who Is Your Real Ideal Customer?

*Just as there are checkpoints in a sales and buying journey, there will be checkpoints through this book to test your learning and application: learning without application is simply entertainment.*

### Ideal Customer Profile Learning

*Were there any "Ah-has" while completing (or reviewing) your ICP? Sometimes it's a single attribute that was missing that turns the 2D image into a 3D (or higher dimensions) view of our ideal, intended prospects. Don't overlook these insights! Remain focused on learning throughout the process and continuously update your ICPs. Also, are you doing everything to find*

> *these people? Or is your pipeline still cluttered with nonideal*
> *prospects? Do the work to declutter and enjoy the feeling of*
> *renewed momentum while also reducing anxiety from mid-*
> *funnel stall risk.*

## A DISCIPLINED APPROACH TO TARGETING

Yes, introducing the concept of the ICP shifts the focus from a broad, undifferentiated approach to a targeted, strategic one.

But having a great set of ICPs and Buyer Personas guarantees nothing.

It's key to step up and maintain discipline against your plan.

**A disciplined approach to how you manage your deals is essential to go from mid-tier to top-performing.**

The case of AirPlus (one of our customers) serves as another beacon shining light on the operational rhythm and efficiency that can be achieved.

Start with a clear understanding and focus on the ICP. Then, add accountability.

AirPlus did this, and it yielded big improvements in their average days to close.

How'd they do it?

This is where mindset matters once again if you are an individual contributor.

Does your manager coach you? Does your manager consistently do consistent pipeline reviews with you? What do they teach?

If you aren't getting these or aren't learning from the reviews, then it's on you to set up that check-in for yourself. Make a scorecard. Do a call review. Schedule weekly pipeline reviews for yourself.

At Airplus, they had (1) salespeople who were clear on their targets, using segmented lists, with a laser focused on particular audiences, *AND* (2) management started to run a disciplined process around pipeline reviews.

These weekly reviews created the operational rhythm to keep those salespeople with clear targeting and time-blocking in a nice flow. More about the importance of this coming up in the next chapter on deal mechanics in the pipeline section.

## BUILD YOUR LIST

It's time to build your list or review the lists you've already created.

As you go through this step by step, consider leveraging a tool in the marketplace. For a list and data enrichment, simply do an online search for "B2B data" or "Sales Intelligence."

**Step 1:** Start by reviewing your ICP. Make any adjustments to it as you read, especially if you haven't visited it recently.

**Step 2:** Then look at your Buyer Personas. Again, make any updates.

**Step 3:** With that done, it's now time to build a list.

One simple way is to use Linked Sales Navigator or a similar tool. Sales Navigator is useful because it shows how many profiles or accounts are active worldwide, with filters for your ICP and preferred buyers by role and region.

Use saved lists to refresh your target lists periodically.

The success of your sales process hinges on targeting the right buyers from the start. Don't waste time casting a wide net. Get clear on your ICP and Buyer Personas today, and watch your sales efforts transform. Your time is too valuable to spend chasing the wrong leads.

## SOUND BYTE SUMMARY

— The ICP and Buyer Personas are the essential first step and puzzle pieces. Don't skip this. Document them carefully and keep them updated with changes you notice in the marketplace.

— They save time by focusing our list-building and prospecting.

— Using an ICP helps sellers focus not on the TAM or the SAM but instead on the SOM.

> To get access to all of the templates, frameworks, tools, and podcast episodes referenced in this book, visit this link: **growthforum.io/bonuses**

## NEXT UP

Once we know which buyers we're targeting and have our lists built, now we can begin tailoring the stages of the deal for them so that they get the information they need at the right time to progress on the deal. This is the time when the system you are building will begin to take shape.

# DEAL MECHANICS

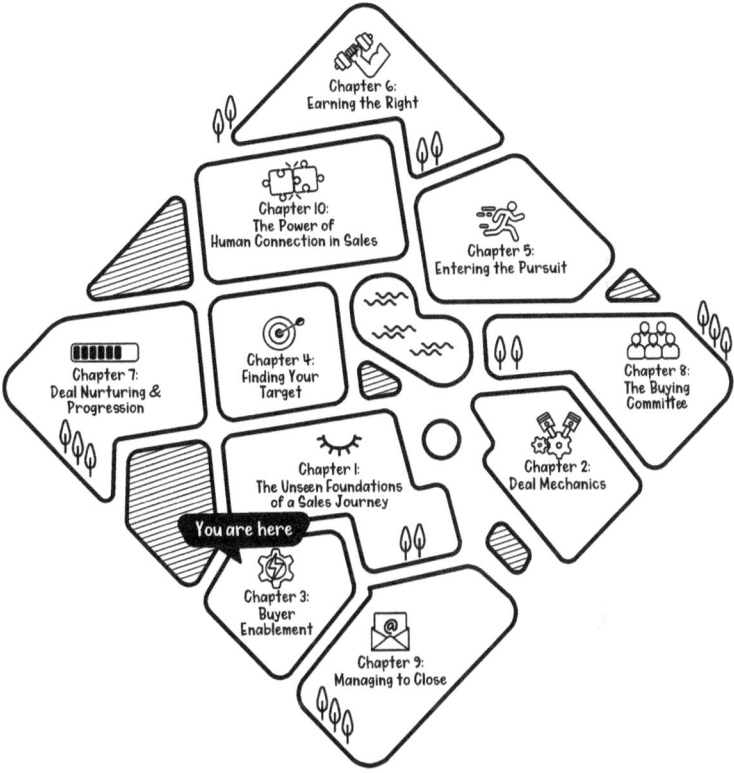

Chapter 6:
Earning the Right

Chapter 10:
The Power of
Human Connection in Sales

Chapter 5:
Entering the Pursuit

Chapter 7:
Deal Nurturing &
Progression

Chapter 4:
Finding Your
Target

Chapter 8:
The Buying
Committee

Chapter 1:
The Unseen Foundations
of a Sales Journey

Chapter 2:
Deal Mechanics

You are here

Chapter 3:
Buyer
Enablement

Chapter 9:
Managing to Close

## The details of *deal mechanics* so that you can give buyers the information they need at every step to progress confidently to decision

Why do some deals stall, while others move swiftly to close? The answer often lies in understanding and mastering the mechanics behind the buyer's journey. Deal mechanics are the roadmap that guides you and your buyer from first conversation to contract signature, ensuring every step is clear, smooth, and effective.

Some salespeople confuse the personal aspect of sales, the human side, with the navigation of the buyer's journey within their organization. The latter refers to the mechanics of a deal. Of course, each conversation, meeting, and step in a process is layered; each interaction is part human and part of the structure.

A sales process is not just the steps to progress a deal. It's about bridging the information gap, and it should *align with the buying process.*

How can you help your buyers open the doors in their organization that need to be opened? (Sometimes, they will have to be made aware of them first.)

When we first started working together, one of our clients, S30 Studios, didn't have its sales stages and processes mapped out.

**Remember: the process is needed before the pursuit can begin.**

Without a clearly defined process, sales efforts become guesswork. A structured sales process not only helps you as the seller but also empowers the buyer, giving them the confidence to move forward with their decision.

Once we mapped it out, their first six-figure deal was done in just eight weeks. Beginner's luck? Or…

The process enables the buyer and the committee to confidently get to a point of decision. The buying process preempts what will be encountered in the deal. Whether it's finance, procurement, or HR, each kind of deal will have a different feel; the buyers will have different needs.

Luke from S30 told us he felt genuine intent from the outset to provide the tools for success, which helped us become an extension of their team while remaining patient with scope and timelines to get a "sh*tload more value than I could have ever hoped for" (in his own words).

The takeaway? A mapped-out sales process doesn't just create efficiency—it speeds up the deal cycle, helping buyers make decisions with confidence. It was a case of putting our Sales OS and V.I.S.I.O.N. Selling Methodology to work, focusing on each deal stage.

Most salespeople use generic stages in a deal pipeline: Prospecting, Discovery, Proposal, and Closed/Won.

This is ours…

Notice how, in the graphic, the cycle begins with connection, then collaboration, and finally commitment, with smaller key steps within those. From this lens, nine steps make up the holistic deal mechanics.

Why is it a circle?

**Because after working with a buyer, they may work with you again, renewing their business or adding on.**

This spiraling energy is common throughout our world and in sales.

Now, keep in mind that buyers may only spend 17% of their buying time with sellers, so the seller needs to make the most of that time and clearly understand where the buyer is in their journey and how that relates to the selling stages.

By the end of this, everything will ideally be connected to your CRM as well. Scripts and frameworks can be connected to each step. (For example, look ahead to Chapter 6: Earning the Right, for a cold-call framework that you can use.)

In today's sales environment, top sellers don't just guide buyers through a process—they enable buyers by providing the right information and tools at each stage. This is what we call buyer enablement (coming up in detail in Chapter 4), and it's critical to each phase of the sales process: Connect, Collaborate, Commit.

Before going into details of each step in the sales process, let's illustrate all of this first at a high level by taking a look at Lui's experience with an international audit and advisory brand.

# ALL THE STEPS IN A DEAL

I once worked on an enterprise deal with 34 people involved in the buying process...

## Connect

It all started by identifying them as a company I wanted to work with. The first engagement was on social media with James on LinkedIn. I asked a few questions—but did *not* connect and pitch-slap.

Instead, I waited, letting it sit.

Then, I shared a podcast insight.

Meanwhile, I was mystery shopping their sales process and their competitors' processes. The first step was to inquire about their website. Right away, I found flaws in the process. (Later, recommendations led to it being fixed, which turned into several million dollars in inbound for that brand.)

## Collaborate

This research meant that in the first meeting, I had and offered a clear point of view. So James said, "Let's have a call with Marketing." The head of Marketing and Head of Digital joined the next one, where I shared my experience with the buying journey. They said, "Amazing, we need to get Frasier involved."

At that meeting, I presented a 15-minute workshop with an ABM lead-scoring module.

Now, with three of his direct reports having endorsed me, the relationship tension was *low* (a very good thing).

It was time to make a business case.

Get this: he asked James and Mary to work with me—"Can you, as a team, start working *together* on the business case?" So I was an external party becoming a part of their team.

To start, the three of us worked together on the discovery analysis document *(business case template—this is part of the bonuses that you can get for free over at growthform.io/bonuses).*

Next, Frasier asked us to present to the Executive team. We did, getting alignment and feedback.

## Commit

Finally, we presented to the Executive team *plus* the group of partners, about 30 people, gaining their agreement and approval.

Preparation and partnership came after that.

Was that the end? No.

The account development process never stops. We are constantly creating, looking, nurturing. That's a holistic approach. That's hard to do if your teams are using an assembly line sales process with handoffs at key stages.

But that is possible if you have a system that allows you to have visibility, input, and ownership of the whole process.

Now, before going deeper into each step of the process, let's consider the context, which centers on a prospect's level of awareness.

## THE FIVE STAGES OF AWARENESS

Let's take a moment to look at what buyers are going through from yet another big picture perspective: do your prospects even know they have a problem?

Sometimes, sellers avoid addressing problems because then they would have to do something. It's better to not know, right? Wrong!

Top sellers are among the best resources for their buyers, particularly when it comes to discovering the root cause of problems and problems that buyers weren't even aware of.

However, there is a *trust* gap. Many buyers simply don't trust sellers. That could be because of a previous bad experience. Every buyer will have varying experiences, expectations, and perceptions of sellers in general. If those memories and engagements are negative, the experience that *you* provide as a seller could buck the normal trend they've seen.

The other aspect of trust comes down to the growth of tech tools and automation. The use of these at scale has led to overwhelm —too many messages and too many that feel like they are automated or even written by AI tools like ChatGPT. (We often do the opposite, write, then have AI assist in editing an email message, for example.)

The overuse of automation means the average buyer receives 147 messages a day across all platforms, and a big percentage of those are ads or lack personalization and relevance.

Do you think buyers care about your quota? Probably not. But they probably do care about their own financials, job security, and reputation. Even if they like a solution, there's still the uncertainty of implementation and whether it will achieve the ROI that you've been selling them.

How do buyers really buy?

There's a simple framework to touch on first, which has to do with *what level of awareness* the buyer has.

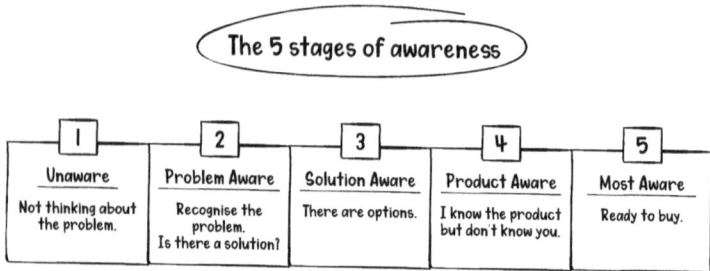

## The 5 stages of awareness

| 1 | 2 | 3 | 4 | 5 |
|---|---|---|---|---|
| Unaware | Problem Aware | Solution Aware | Product Aware | Most Aware |
| Not thinking about the problem. | Recognise the problem. Is there a solution? | There are options. | I know the product but don't know you. | Ready to buy. |

Stage 1—Unaware: Not thinking about the problem

Stage 2—Problem Aware: Recognize the problem. Is there a solution?

Stage 3—Solution Aware: There are options.

Stage 4—Product Aware: I know the product but don't know you.

Stage 5—Most Aware: Ready to buy.

Recognizing where each of your buyers are in the five stages of awareness will help meet them where they are, start conversations, begin to collaborate, and then get them to a point of decision.

### Stage 1—Unaware: Not Thinking About the Problem

Characteristics:

- At this stage, buyers don't recognize that they have a specific need or problem that requires a solution.
- They are essentially oblivious to the issues that the product addresses or the potential improvements it could bring to their life or business.

Strategies:

- Educational content
- Awareness campaigns
- Direct outreach

### Stage 2—Problem Aware: Recognize the Problem. Is There a Solution?

Characteristics:

- The buyer is now aware that they face an issue or a challenge that needs addressing.
- This awareness might come from experiencing pain points, noticing inefficiencies, or through external influences such as discussions, research, or competitor comparisons.

Strategies:

- Blog content for search engine discovery, i.e., SEO
- Social proof (review websites like G2, Google Reviews, etc.)
- Tools
  - → Content marketing
  - → Buyer intent tools
  - → Social listening tools like Brandwatch

### Stage 3—Solution Aware: There Are Options

Characteristics:

- The buyer knows that solutions exist and starts to explore the various options available.
- They are gathering detailed information about each potential solution to compare their features, benefits, and drawbacks.

Strategies:

- Product information
- Comparison tools
- Customer reviews

## Stage 4—Product Aware:
## I Know the Product but Don't Know You

Characteristics:

- The buyer knows about your product and its basic functions but hasn't yet formed a deep understanding of how it compares to alternatives or how it could specifically benefit them.

Strategies:

- Brand storytelling
- Customer success stories
- Content marketing

## Stage 5—Most Aware: Ready to Buy

Characteristics:

- The buyer has all the information they need and is in the process of finalizing their purchase decision.
- They may be comparing final details and costs or considering the terms of sale.

Strategies:

- Simple buying process
- Personalized communication
- Customer support

Recognizing where each of your buyers are in the five stages of awareness will help meet them where they are, start conversations, begin to collaborate, and then work through all objections to get them to a confident point of decision.

As we move into the next section, consider how awareness affects the different stages of the selling and buying process.

## THE 3 CS— CONNECT, COLLABORATE, COMMIT

When I was recently buying carpet for my home renovation, I asked the salesperson what the difference was between the two carpets. One was $65 a foot, and the other was $85.

His response was "Price."

"Really? I could already see that."

Contrast that with the next salesperson at a different store who sat me down and *showed* me the difference in material, which justified the price difference. I stopped him midway through his education: "I'm going to buy from you."

He also didn't try to upsell me on the expensive option, reasoning that the carpet would be in a low-traffic area of my home and wouldn't be fit for purpose.

The next day, I had a 9 a.m. meeting, so I had to show up at his store earlier than they opened. He met me there and easily organized the delivery.

The complete experience we create for buyers is about educating, guiding, and nurturing. People remember how you make them feel.

It's then critical to facilitate the flow of information at each stage so they have exactly what they want and need to confidently get to a point of decision.

Each of the larger stages—Connect, Collaborate, and Commit—has three stages within them, for nine total stages.

Let's take the big three—one at a time.

## CONNECT

Overlaying the Five Stages of Awareness onto the above, it can be seen that Connect is where we want to get an impression of where the buyer is and then set them on a track to increase their awareness.

You have defined your ICP and created a list based on the ICP attributes. Now, you are reaching out and engaging with your target. This stage is all about creating awareness and starting a conversation.

The connect stage is also about earning the right to start a conversation. To progress a conversation there needs to be an element of trust. Relationship tension must be reduced to allow your prospect to open up and share their opposition with you.

Connect is also about engagement. It's not a one-way conversation. We are leveraging the different channels to start a conversation. If an inbound lead asks for information, we are asking what motivated them to ask for that, how long they've been considering, and why now.

Remember, only 17% of the time spent buying is spent with a salesperson. Once you have engagement, use the time wisely.

It all begins with the target list—there is much more on this in Chapter 4: Finding Your Target, where we'll lay out the steps to building your ICP(s) and Buyer Persona(s).

Prospecting is obviously critical because it creates awareness among buyers about you and what you offer.

Skills that come into play here are research and personalization.

Research doesn't have to take long, but it is necessary because it enables personalization.

VanillaSoft asked decision-makers what they expect when sellers contact them for a meeting. 88% said they expected sellers to know them, their industry, and their problems, along with insight into those.

Show them you know them, then engage. Then, determine if you are a good fit for them and if they are for you.

Now, a brief word on where your prospects will come from...

## Outbound vs. Inbound

Why even consider outbound when an inbound funnel could be "turned on" with a paid ad campaign on social media platforms? It's a good question.

The reality is you will do both. However...

*We are big fans of outbound because it is proactive, predictable, and 100% in your control.*

This is because successful targeting in outbound can also increase inbound.

You save time by focusing only on the list you have made. These people fit into the ideal customer profile, and your Buyer Personas help you provide a lot of value during outbound.

I'm such an advocate of outbound, phone-led prospecting that I did an experiment with P3 Recovery for prospective franchisees and found that a cold-calling approach led to significantly lower-cost first meetings than an alternative approach that most usually fall into the trap of doing due to its allure of *"easiness."* That case study is coming up in Chapter 5: Entering the Pursuit.

The other consideration is that there is only a small percentage of buyers that are actually ready to buy right now. Therefore, it's important to create awareness about who you are *before* those buyers get to that point of decision because by that time, they're probably working with another salesperson.

That's an extra 25% of the market that you can get the attention of. Some of them may never have become aware of the problems you can help with if not for your engagement with them.

## COLLABORATE

This is the part where buyer enablement truly kicks in (more on that in Chapter 4: Buyer Enablement). How helpful can you be as you discover, align, and present?

Collaboration works when we take what we've learned about our buyers and help them develop a solution that will have an impact.

Collaboration is not just ticking the boxes in our sales process. It is about continuously giving value, nurturing, and educating while taking key action steps like developing the business case and presenting to the Buying Committee for consensus.

We are now learning where the buyer is in their buying journey and what is happening in their business. Has anything changed recently? The answer to this gives you insight into the thought process the buyer is taking and also might be a clue toward an opportunity for transformational change.

In the first conversation with Frasier, the relationship tension was very low because of the three endorsements from his direct reports. That allowed us to speak openly to understand what they faced and where we might find alignment.

### The First Conversation

Another way of thinking about the sales process is as a series of commitments. We see six major stages, the first of which usually happens in the Discovery phase.

The six stages of commitment are:

1. Time (the first sales conversation) → In Chapter 7, we are going to show you how to run this first meeting
2. Get them to share information
3. Collaboration
4. Consensus
5. Change
6. Commitment to budget

**The Six Stages of Commitment**

| | |
|---|---|
| 1 | Time (the first sales conversation) |
| 2 | Get them to share information |
| 3 | Collaboration |
| 4 | Consensus |
| 5 | Change |
| 6 | Commitment to budget |

Once you're in a conversation or a meeting, getting them to share information could unlock a great trusted advisor relationship. A question that shows you are interested in something they've had to change in, say, the last six months might engage them in a way others haven't. Keep looking for ways to get them to share, even if that means adding one or two warmup questions to your repertoire (*"Before we start the meeting,* I'd love to know xx...").

This stage is about deepening your understanding of the prospect's needs, challenges, and objectives. It's an investigative process. By asking the right questions, a tailored scope of action can be created.

Remember that the discovery phase is crucial for establishing trust and demonstrating your commitment to solving the client's specific problems. Trust is everything in sales—before product quality, before giving value at *every* stage, before the sales process, before pricing—before anyone buys, they have to trust you.

Discovery never ends. Keep in mind the value of staying curious throughout the buyer journey.

We'll talk more about Discovery in Chapter 4: Buyer Enablement.

## COMMIT

The culmination of your efforts is the commitment phase, where negotiation and commitment happen. This step involves addressing any remaining concerns, finalizing terms, and securing the agreement.

A successful close is the result of effectively managing all previous steps—giving value at *every* stage—ensuring that the solution perfectly aligns with the client's needs and expectations.

It's critical to address any objections—especially hidden objections. (More about this in Chapter 9.)

Closing sets up the onboarding stages to make sure that the buyer gets all the value promised by the solution.

## WHAT IF I ALREADY HAVE A SALES SYSTEM?

Maybe you already have a sales system.

It's likely you do (in a manner of speaking).

Whatever activities, patterns, behaviors, and approaches to sales and marketing you have amounts to a system.

It just may not be formalized. Without formalizing it, it can devolve into hope as a strategy.

Usually, there are one of three routes to working on your sales system:

1. Tweaking
2. Reshaping
3. Building from scratch

**Tweaking:** You may simply be making minor changes to the structure and inputs of what you've got. Sometimes, small fixes make a big difference. For instance, when applying the system while at Locomote, Dave didn't see the results he was looking for at first. After Lui took a look, he diagnosed that the messaging wasn't quite right.

We were leading with cost and better experience when the real problem at the time was being compliant and looking after staff once COVID-19 restrictions started to ease.

Instead, we started asking questions like "When people start traveling again, will you be ready?"

When we started getting calls, it felt easy. Because the main components of the system were already in place, adjusting the messaging was more of a tweak than anything else.

**Reshaping:** It's also possible you're open to reshaping your system quite dramatically. That's all good. It will take an investment of time and energy, but with a growth mindset and a goal in mind, we'll help you get there.

**Building from scratch:** We do this with individuals and teams coming into Growth Forum every week.

It's likely your sales system will be tweaked, reshaped, and even built from scratch at some point in your sales life because sales is an infinite game.

### Checkpoint 3:
### Building Blocks to Your Sales Process

*Just as there are checkpoints in a sales and buying journey, there will be checkpoints through this book to test your learning and application: learning without application is simply entertainment.*

### Sales Process Foundation Stones

*Which of the three phases are you doing best in? Which of the nine stages within those three phases needs the most improvement?*

## IT'S TIME TO BUILD YOUR SALES PROCESS

A sales process is not just about the steps you need to tick to progress a deal.

How will you bridge the information gap buyers and the Buying Committee have within each step?

A well-defined sales process enables the sale. It should align with the steps the buyers need to take to progress. Remember that you know how to sell what you're selling; it's key to find ways to facilitate the buying process because the buyer often will not fully understand their own organization, such as how they purchase, nor necessarily how to open the right doors.

The tactical elements of your system will be built around the structure of that step-by-step process.

*This is your chance to begin building out your system.*

*Tip: You're not alone! Bring your questions to the Growth Forum community.*

Start by mapping out the steps required to move a prospect from the initial contact to the final sale…for *your* product or service in light of their buying journey and awareness.

Take a look at the nine steps in the image once more…

Next, consider again the Five Stages of Awareness.

The 5 stages of awareness

| 1 | 2 | 3 | 4 | 5 |
|---|---|---|---|---|
| Unaware | Problem Aware | Solution Aware | Product Aware | Most Aware |
| Not thinking about the problem. | Recognise the problem. Is there a solution? | There are options. | I know the product but don't know you. | Ready to buy. |

Now we're going to layer on top of this what the buyer needs to know to progress…

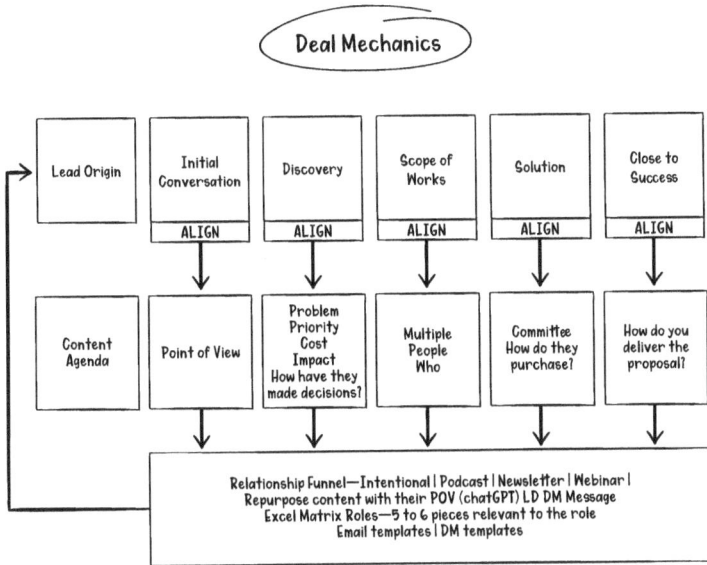

## Deal Mechanics

| Lead Origin | Initial Conversation | Discovery | Scope of Works | Solution | Close to Success |
|---|---|---|---|---|---|
| | ALIGN | ALIGN | ALIGN | ALIGN | ALIGN |
| Content Agenda | Point of View | Problem Priority Cost Impact How have they made decisions? | Multiple People Who | Committee How do they purchase? | How do you deliver the proposal? |

Relationship Funnel—Intentional | Podcast | Newsletter | Webinar | Repurpose content with their POV (chatGPT) LD DM Message Excel Matrix Roles—5 to 6 pieces relevant to the role Email templates | DM templates

Information is knowledge. Knowledge is power. Therefore, information is power.

Make sure the prospect has the information they need to empower them!

Using the notes below, begin to build out each step in *your* process. This may be a continuation of the steps you already began to map out earlier in the chapter. If you haven't already, now's your chance.

You will see we included an example from P3 Recovery of how we have taken action on each of these steps.

# Connect (Goal + Action Steps)

## Prospect

1. Goal: Creating awareness for who you are combined with a perspective to make it easier to start a conversation
2. Action steps:
   a. Various ways to make people learn about you (content, ads, etc.)
   b. Use completed ICP/Buyer Personas—know the type of people you want to work with and plan how to attract them
   c. List(s) built and updated; focus on leads that are ICP, remove clutter from lists
3. Example from P3 Recovery: New *customized* inquiry email sent when a new lead meets criteria (e.g., someone familiar with ice baths versus a customer who isn't)

## Engage

1. Goal: Lower relationship tension so that you can have a great conversation because of the trust that is beginning to be built
2. Action steps:
   a. Demonstrate professionalism by understanding the level of awareness the buyer has
   b. Provide initial insight to tackle problems they may be facing
   c. Map out how value will be given throughout the buying experience by giving relevant education upfront
3. Example from P3 Recovery: Call the prospect

### Qualify

1. Goal: Find out if there is a problem to tackle and then book regular meetings for Discovery (the next stage)
2. Action steps:
   a. Right-fit prospect in the right conversations (buyers are qualifying sellers while we are qualifying them)
   b. Is it a problem worth investigating further? Sometimes, one buyer's fire is just one of seven fires their executive can see, and that fire may be manageable and not a priority (ask questions to learn this).
   c. Time-block to ensure cadence is effective; use pre-call planner; review engaged prospects against initial ICP/ Buyer Personas to ensure good fit; post-call follow-up
3. Example from P3 Recovery: If a good fit, a calendar invite is sent

## Collaborate (Goal + Action Steps)

### Discovery

1. Goal: To find the best-fit buyers to proceed
2. Action steps:
   a. Ask questions to learn must-haves for progression
   b. Past-based questions help to uncover what changed to drive the current motivation
   c. Is this problem something the buyer truly wants to rectify (future state) and is willing to go on a journey to do that?
3. Example from P3 Recovery: Learn what prompted the prospect to reach out and why they want to become part of the P3 network now. Do they have the ingredients to go through the whole process of starting a franchise?

### Align

1. Goal: Fill knowledge gaps and build awareness and general feasibility about the solution
2. Action steps:
   a. Give, nurture, and educate during business case development
   b. Review the proposal from the buyer's perspective to earn the right to progress
3. Example from P3 Recovery: Review financial template

### Present

1. Goal: Starting to build consensus in the buying committee
2. Action steps:
   a. Ensure each step in the sales process is complete before progressing
   b. Follow a cadence of information delivery to keep buyers engaged
3. Example from P3 Recovery: Use a prospect application to tailor a presentation

## Commit (Goal + Action Steps)

### Agree

1. Goal: Finding buying committee consensus on the solution
2. Action steps:
   a. The business case fully buttoned up through the champion and all of the buying stakeholders
   b. Check-ins to develop consensus
3. Example from P3 Recovery: Contract preparation

### Prepare

1. Goal: Develop a plan to execute the solution
2. Action steps:
   a. Feasibility plan built into roadmap
   b. Resources required for feasibility arranged
3. Example from P3 Recovery: Onboarding plans made

### Partner

1. Goal: Follow through on commitment to give value and continue building trust
2. Action steps:
   a. Onboarding into the sold solution
   b. Customer service brings value throughout onboarding
3. Example from P3 Recovery: Execute the onboarding process

## Helping the Buyer Gain Confidence

Remember, the primary objective of this process is to enable the buyer to go through each stage and reduce the risk that the buyer will detour to No Decision based on not having the confidence to move forward.

1. **Confidence:** We want to do this—a great level of intent—but don't believe in the ability to execute (can be conditioned by previous experiences and biases).
2. **Information gap:** We want to go ahead, but there are some missing pieces. (This is why we seek understanding before progressing—What concerns do you have based on what we've shared so far?)
3. **Lack of Consensus:** We really want to do this but don't have consensus within the Buying Committee. (The lure of self-interest kicks in.)

You can see the deal mechanics we've outlined are a combination of the sales process and the buying journey.

Tailor these stages to best reflect your specific business and sales process.

Each stage should have specific goals and actions associated with it, ensuring that your team is clear on what needs to be accomplished at each step.

Here's a few additional ideas to consider...

## Establishing Key Performance Indicators (KPIs)

KPIs are metrics that help you measure and evaluate the effectiveness of your sales pipeline.

Identify the key metrics that indicate progress and success at each stage.

These could include:

- Number of Leads Generated
- Conversion Rates
- Average Deal Size
- Sales Cycle Length

Monitoring these KPIs allows you to identify trends, spot potential issues, and make data-driven decisions to optimize your sales performance. It's this feedback that might prompt changes in your system as well.

## Customer Relationship Management Tools (CRMs)

Thanks to technological advancements, heaps of CRM tools are available to streamline your sales process.

These tools help you track and manage your leads, automate repetitive tasks, and provide insights into your pipeline performance.

Make sure to:

- Choose a tool that aligns with your specific needs and integrates seamlessly with your existing systems
- Learn how to effectively use these tools to maximize their productivity and efficiency

### Reviewing and Updating Your Pipeline

Set aside dedicated time (block time out in your calendar) to review your sales pipeline regularly.

**The pipeline needs to reflect reality as much as possible.**

Assess each prospect's progress, identify any bottlenecks or issues, and make necessary adjustments to your sales process to keep your pipeline flowing smoothly.

Pay attention to the feedback prospects give you.

Update your sales stages, processes, and KPIs regularly to reflect the evolving needs of your business and customers. Your sales process should align with the buying process and be tailored to give customers the information they need when they need it.

### Overcoming Common Sales Pipeline Challenges

Building and managing a sales pipeline can be challenging, and obstacles may arise along the way.

Common challenges include inconsistent lead quality, long sales cycles, and difficulty in accurately forecasting revenue.

To overcome these challenges, focus on:

- Continuously improving your lead generation strategies
- Refining your qualification criteria
- Taking time for self-coaching where improvement is possible

Regularly analyze your pipeline data to identify areas for optimization and implement changes to address any issues that arise.

Remember, building a successful sales pipeline takes time, dedication, and continuous refinement.

Implementing the strategies outlined in this chapter can help you lay a solid foundation for your sales process, which will have a positive impact on your pipeline, giving you better chances to achieve sustainable growth.

## SOUND BYTE SUMMARY

— Determine your sales process, noting the details and KPIs in each step.

— Ensure your sales operating system has quality inputs, leading to better outputs, such as fewer No Decisions, faster cycles, or more closed/won deals.

To get access to all of the templates, frameworks, tools, and podcast episodes referenced in this book, visit this link: **growthforum.io/bonuses**

## NEXT UP

The buyer journey is increasingly complex. Buyer enablement is about putting yourself in the buyer's shoes to truly help them by bringing value at every stage of their journey.

# BUYER ENABLEMENT

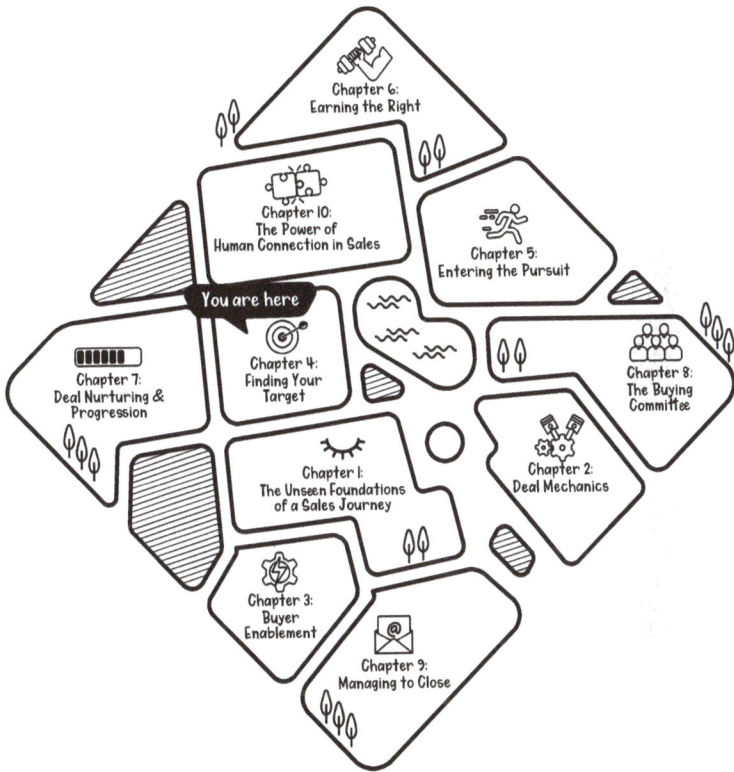

Chapter 6:
Earning the Right

Chapter 10:
The Power of
Human Connection in Sales

Chapter 5:
Entering the Pursuit

You are here

Chapter 7:
Deal Nurturing &
Progression

Chapter 4:
Finding Your
Target

Chapter 8:
The Buying
Committee

Chapter 1:
The Unseen Foundations
of a Sales Journey

Chapter 2:
Deal Mechanics

Chapter 3:
Buyer
Enablement

Chapter 9:
Managing to Close

## The finer points of *buyer enablement* in the increasingly complex buyer journey.

E ver wonder why deals stall even when you're sure you've done everything right? The answer often lies in the missing pieces of the buyer's journey—pieces only you, the seller, can help them discover. This is where buyer enablement comes in. It's not just about selling a product; it's about guiding your buyers through a complex decision-making process, ensuring they have the information, confidence, and clarity to move forward.

Imagine working on a complex puzzle; each piece must be carefully selected and placed with precision. It's not about forcing pieces to fit or hastily assembling them. Instead, the art lies in patiently gathering the right elements and aligning them powerfully in the correct order.

In the previous chapter, we showed you this image...

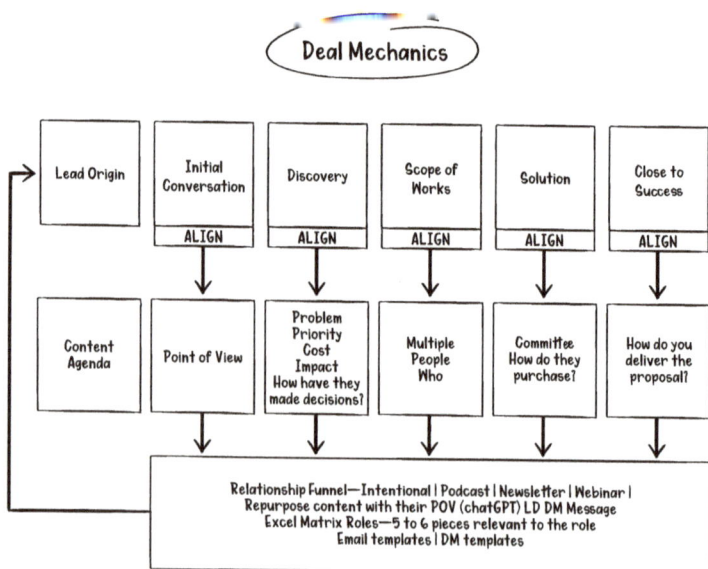

**Deal Mechanics**

| Lead Origin | Initial Conversation | Discovery | Scope of Works | Solution | Close to Success |
|---|---|---|---|---|---|
| ALIGN | ALIGN | ALIGN | ALIGN | ALIGN | ALIGN |
| Content Agenda | Point of View | Problem Priority Cost Impact How have they made decisions? | Multiple People Who | Committee How do they purchase? | How do you deliver the proposal? |

Relationship Funnel—Intentional | Podcast | Newsletter | Webinar | Repurpose content with their POV (chatGPT) LD DM Message Excel Matrix Roles—5 to 6 pieces relevant to the role Email templates | DM templates

Just like deal mechanics, Buyer Enablement involves setting up pieces in the right order.

Do you know the top concerns, priorities, and beliefs your buyers have?

If yes, how do you learn those?

If no, how will you?

These concerns, priorities, and beliefs can change primarily during the Connection phase (referring back to Chapter 3: Deal Mechanics) as one gets into the Collaboration phase and learns more.

In fact, as one becomes a trusted advisor *through* buyer enablement—giving value at every stage—it's more likely that you'll discover or simply be told what those concerns, priorities, and beliefs are in plain English.

We've found that Sales OS helps with **buyer enablement**.

Buyer enablement, defined another way, is the process of providing your buyers with the tools, information, and guidance they need to make informed, confident decisions. Its essence is reducing friction at every stage of the buying journey and helping buyers see the clear path from problem to solution.

One of the products we are testing Sales OS on is in one of the most challenging and saturated markets out there—the health franchise space. The sales cycle average is 90–120 days, at best. Yet two deals early on closed in 27 and 28 days. We credit this to updating the buyer enablement strategy.

Just like the seller, the buyer is on a journey. The seller seeks to discover what gaps may exist in the buyer's understanding of content, information, and ROI frameworks. Objections aid in this process. Great sellers listen and learn about buyers' reservations and then address them proactively, *enabling* them at every stage of the deal.

The result? Instead of seeing your pipeline cluster at typical stall points, buyers will move smoothly over those hurdles. Even if they don't, your system will be adaptable and provide you, as the seller, with the chance to learn from the buyer and perhaps deliver unexpected value.

It may feel like a drag to learn what your buyer is going through, but it's actually the best use of your time once you've upped your mindset.

In this chapter, you'll learn the details of buyer enablement and how to use the tools we've used to improve your own processes.

Where is buyer enablement happening in terms of phases and stages of the deal?

**It's happening in most, if not all of the stages.**

In the Introduction, we discussed that buyers don't buy the features and benefits of what you're selling but the outcome you help them to achieve. One goal is to *avoid* No Decision outcomes, which, according to some studies, is up to 40–60% in B2B sales.

In this chapter, we will talk about how to enable buyers to better see those outcomes and, more often, end up closed/won.

To do that, we'll start by unpacking how buyers approach their buying decisions.

Of course, playing *defense* to avoid No Decision could put you in a scarcity mindset. From an abundance mindset, deals that you and your clients didn't even imagine come suddenly into view like seeds popping out of the soil.

The experience with News Corp is a perfect example of how buyer enablement—understanding and validating the buyer's needs, then guiding them with insight—leads to far greater results than just pushing for a sale.

## UNDERSTANDING YOUR BUYERS' JOURNEY CAN UNLOCK A BIGGER DEAL

Sometimes, there's a deal on the table that is right there for the taking. It might even be the best deal your company has ever made. The business case validation is done, and not just the champion but the *entire* buying committee is ready. Should you take it?

That depends.

In this chapter, we want you to learn that a foundation must be laid and improved upon for you to enter into these kinds of negotiations, with your boss, with buyers, and with *yourself.*

At its heart is this theme of buyer enablement. If we are truly looking at the world from the other person's view, then we'll be able to meld our approach to seek value together and speak in an engaging and inviting manner in search of it.

There very well might be a deal your client, even your boss, with all their experience and wisdom, cannot see. Why not?

Maybe it's because they have a different perspective from you.

Have you shared what you've learned from your unique vantage?

The ability to share this comes from different lenses. The lens of experience. The lens of new eyes. The lens of data. The lens of the customer. How we've done things before. How we *could* do things today or tomorrow. Ask, "What if?"

## News Corp: Lui's First Eight-Figure Deal

At News Corp, instead of rushing to close a $500k deal, I took the time to observe their operations and validate suspicions they already had. This patience turned what could have been a modest deal into an eight-figure one, and it all happened because I focused on enabling the buyer to understand their own business better. That's the power of buyer enablement—offering insights that the buyer can't see on their own and then guiding them to a much bigger, more valuable solution. Here's how it went down…

I'll never forget when I asked Marcus of News Corp whether it'd be okay if I observed their factory operations.

Moments before, I'd entered the massive foyer of their headquarters. An impressive etched metal portrait watched over me as I checked in. Soon, I was in Marcus's office.

To even get this meeting, I leveraged a referral, got the phone number, and called until I got through. There was already a bit of tension in our conversation by the time I popped the question. But he lowered his glasses and said, "Sure."

So for two weeks, every night, I showed up at 11:30 p.m., watched the printing come alive by 2:30 a.m., and watched the papers go out the door by 4:30 a.m.

Even though my boss wanted me to close a $500k deal that was already on the table, which would have been our company's biggest to date, I held him off while I gathered observations in the early hours at the factory. The notes I jotted are still in a binder on my shelf—man, that was fun!

I went back to Marcus and shared my findings.

These insights led me to become Marcus's trusted advisor because I was able to confirm suspicions he already had. Soon, I was added to his internal team. That turned into a task force to prepare a different, larger deal.

With teams in Australia and America we developed a razor-thin business case—simple and to the point—but the final business case didn't have my name or my company's name on it because it had to be sold internally.

That was a deal that succeeded because I validated what Marcus had suspected about the business. And because I was there in service of News Corp as the customer, instead of settling for the $500k deal that my boss wanted and was begging me to close. We skipped from six to eight figures.

**The 20x of the original deal size was nice, of course, but the learning was the key: patiently adding value in discovery, achieving trusted advisor status, and selling internally.**

My next eight-figure deal was twice the size and took only half the time.

As this deal gradually developed, what allowed me to keep going? I think, above all, it was my mindset, which kept me in a curious and tenacious state of mind. Of course, I didn't know how it was going to turn out. The only way to find out was to keep going, continue providing value, and keep the faith.

*For more details on this deal and buyer-seller relationships, check out the interview with Marcus in the Bonus Chapter at the end of the book.*

## SALES IS A GAME ABOUT CHANGE

In the Introduction, we talked about sales as a simple, infinite game.

It can also be described as a game about *change*, because that is what sales is behind the curtain.

People don't buy what you do. They buy your help in their journey toward some type of change in their business. **Change is the outcome you help them achieve.**

How will your buyer's life change, and how will it be different once they've completed their buyer's journey? How do you plan to facilitate that?

Many say change is hard. (Even though staying the same is often harder on you.) And the cost of inaction is often tougher for a company's bottom line. Often internal debates, in the buyer's mind and with their Buying Committee, is the psychology underpinning hesitancy in a deal.

On the good side of change, they may describe it as a solution, as a business case, as ROI, as an improvement in efficiency, and much more.

If someone is paying, they aren't buying the status quo.

**They want to buy change.**

Even though they may have some anxiety about how to proceed.

On the one hand, the buying journey is similar to how it has always been.

It starts with a problem. What kind of problem exactly? Once that's decided, solutions can be explored. Sometimes that exploration opens back up the discussion about what the problem is.

As solutions start to come into the picture, requirements building begins. Again, there can be overlap and back and forth between the solution exploration and requirements building phases.

Finally, to round out this typical B2B decision-making flow, a supplier is selected, the purchase is made, and it's on to implementation, often the trickiest part. (If you are a true facilitator, discussions about implementation and onboarding will start in Discovery.)

## Do Buyers Really Need Sellers?

Recently, we were being sold a CRM option. Instead of asking what challenge we were currently trying to tackle, the salesperson went straight to the demo. Not a good use of the time.

With interactions like this, it's no wonder many buyers prefer not to work with a seller. Or they only work with one when nearing the transaction; perhaps they've already secured a budget and it's decision time.

Again, this isn't a criticism of buyers; it's a wake-up call for sellers.

Most people we've coached are founders and sales teams who don't just want short-term wins. They also don't want to rely on chance, luck, or fate.

They want repeatable results—sales relationships that lead to positive outcomes in line with their promises and relationships to go along with those results that lead to referrals.

Not only that, but many of them want to stay at the top of their game for a long time.

They want help in becoming the sellers that buyers want to work with.

No matter where in the B2B space you are, the principles are the same. Buyers need to get to a point of confidence. Confidence doesn't mean there's no risk. It just means they understand and see the ROI that's possible, too.

They need to say, "Yes, I can see value in this. I've got confidence that this can work."

By the way, the same goes for business-to-consumer (B2C): a consumer might need to talk to their partner, while a business might need to talk to their executive team.

B2B usually involves more people who we have to get on board for some kind of change or solution—stakeholders, decision influencers, what we call the Buying Committee. More people means more steps, but it's the *same* **decision flow**.

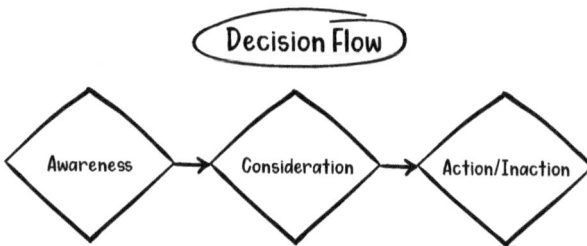

Simplified further from the Five Stages of Awareness, we are bringing buyers from unawareness (not thinking about the problem) to problem aware (recognizing the problem), to solution aware (there are options), to product aware (I know the product, but I don't know you), to the most aware (ready to buy).

Just because the buying journey is complex doesn't mean sales facilitation can't be simple, but it does lead to one unfortunately major outcome if the buying journey isn't navigated properly.

## THE COMPLEX BUYING JOURNEY

The B2B buying journey is as complex as it's ever been.

It used to look something like this: moving from Problem Identification to Solution Exploration to Requirements Building to Supplier Selection to Purchase Decision.

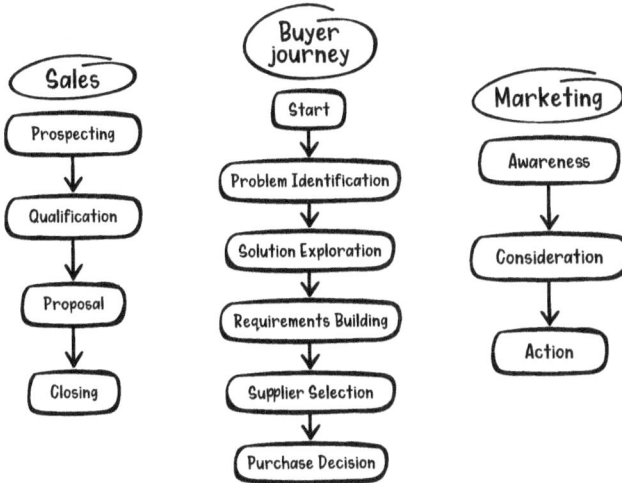

**Sales**
- Prospecting
- Qualification
- Proposal
- Closing

**Buyer journey**
- Start
- Problem Identification
- Solution Exploration
- Requirements Building
- Supplier Selection
- Purchase Decision

**Marketing**
- Awareness
- Consideration
- Action

Now it's a bit more like this, adapted from Gartner...

**Complex B2B Buying Journey**

Within each step of the journey, there are multiple questions, multiple pieces of information, and multiple sources for that information. Conversations occur in a variety of venues, online and face to face, between the buying team and the sellers.

Sometimes, new insights send the buyer backward in the process. For example, during "Solution Exploration," the buyer downloads a white paper. The questions posed in that white paper make the buyer think, *Maybe I'm not yet focusing on the right problem* or *There's more to this problem than I first thought.*

Those thoughts send the buyer *backward* to "Problem Identification." This time, though, the buyer is more aware of the depth or scope of the problem. Therefore, it's a good reason to take a step back and then continue the process. It's better to return to "Problem Identification" from "Solution Exploration" than to go all the way back to the day of the "Purchase Decision."

### Navigator

One more analogy to consider to clarify your role as a salesperson:

Imagine a crowded nightclub, and you're carrying a tray of drinks from the bar to a table where your friends are waiting. The path is full of obstacles. At any moment, someone could bump you, and the drinks could spill everywhere.

Now, reimagine this scenario with a twist: You're equipped with an earpiece, and from a balcony above, you're the guide offering the walker clear, calm directions. With each step, you must provide updates and alerts—give, educate, nurture.

Sometimes, the crowd thins here or gets dense there, so a reroute is needed.

Help your teammate (the buyer) avoid collisions, navigate the crowds, and reach their destination without spilling a drop.

Cheers!

## NO DECISION IS COMMON, BUT IT DOESN'T HAVE TO BE YOUR NORM

Because of increased complexity, 40–60% of deals with buyers that sellers speak to end in *No Decision*.

That's about *half*.

It doesn't have to be this way—for you—as you develop your system.

The biggest reason for No Decision? The business case isn't spot on.

The business case hasn't been communicated, codeveloped, and understood by the buyer. Remember, it's the salesperson's role to facilitate this conversation. Leaving this up to the champion in the Buying Committee often isn't enough.

Yes, it can be that there's an internal champion who can get things done. Then, it's the buyer who just needs to ask, "What do you need?" and get that to the champion who makes things happen. At every stage of the deal, the seller needs to make sure the value is clear for progression to occur. Not doing this can lead to No Decision. That's a lot of time spent for nothing to happen.

In the case of No Decision, the buyer, the Buying Committee, and the company are sometimes saying that while they do have a pain point and recognize your solution would solve it, they would rather not go through with the pain of change to get there.

In other words, in that case, they've decided the cost of inaction is less than the return on investment. It could be they know the cost of inaction while the return on investment carries too much risk, which devalues it.

**Ultimately, it's the business case and implementation plan that together drive value and aid the Buying Committee in coming to an informed, confident decision.**

If salespeople succeed in becoming the ones the Buying Committee trusts to develop that business case, then the potential for a successful close increases, and the greater the chances the buyers have of enjoying the ROI post-implementation.

## WHEN DO BUYERS ENGAGE SELLERS?

According to Chet Holmes, about 3% of buyers are actively looking for what you're selling. Perhaps 6% to 7% are open to it. There's another 30% not thinking about it. Thirty percent don't think they're interested. And the last 30% know they're not interested.

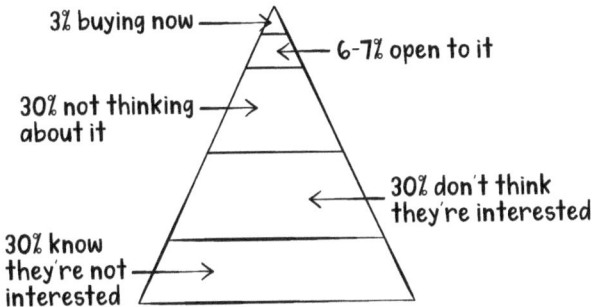

Now, of that 3% that are actively looking—that are buying now—many will wait until they are already beyond awareness and through the consideration stage, entering the decision stage *before* engaging with sellers.

If they've waited that long, what are the chances they'll reach out to you?

If they've never heard of you, you might get lucky and reach out to them at the right time. However, Sales OS encourages you to engage with buyers much earlier during the awareness phase. At times, you will even reach out to buyers with value in the pre-awareness phase. This way, it's you who can nurture them up through awareness, consideration, and perhaps all the way to the point of decision.

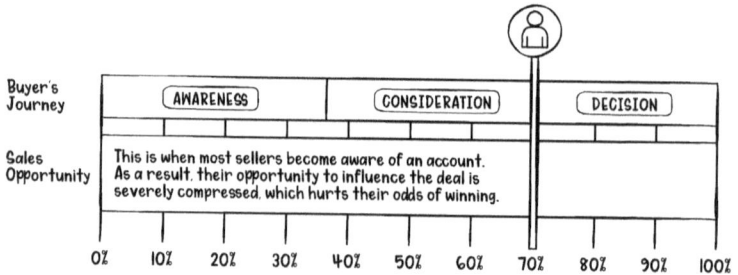

| Buyer's Journey | AWARENESS | | | | CONSIDERATION | | | DECISION | | |
|---|---|---|---|---|---|---|---|---|---|---|

Sales Opportunity: This is when most sellers become aware of an account. As a result, their opportunity to influence the deal is severely compressed, which hurts their odds of winning.

0%  10%  20%  30%  40%  50%  60%  70%  80%  90%  100%

This is where your marketing hat goes on. How can buyers become aware of you sooner? Simple. By you creating value for them. We'll expand on this as the chapter progresses.

Another way of thinking about this: which journey is longer, the buyer's or the seller's?

It's the buyer's journey.

And yet it is the seller who knows what the roadmap looks like for what the seller is offering. It's the seller who can help facilitate. Otherwise, the buyer and Buying Committee will try to lay out the roadmap themselves instead of understanding what you as the seller have typically seen with previous successful buyers.

Referring again to the image, the seller can expand their own journey to go alongside the buyer to help them become aware of their problems before they cost their business too much or to help them envision even better ways to help their customers.

## Checkpoint 4:
## Where Do Buyers Get Information?

*Just as there are checkpoints in a sales and buying journey, there will be checkpoints through this book to test your learning and application: learning without application is simply entertainment.*

### From Search Engines to Trusted Advisors

*It's not only search engines, but the buying journey that has changed. Have you changed the way you humbly but insightfully engage with your audience? Try surveying your audience to find out where they get their info when trying to find solutions to their problems. Find out what info they need to confidently progress through the buying journey. Know your audience and what's important to them.*

# CREATING CONTENT MARKETING FOCUSED ON EFFICIENCY

In the fast-paced marketing world, efficiency isn't just a buzzword—it's a necessity. The pressure is on to produce high-quality content that resonates with your audience without wasting time or resources. Sit around and you'd eat the dust of your peers.

But how do you achieve maximum efficiency? How do you make it so no time or effort is wasted? The key lies in understanding your target audience deeply and creating content that speaks directly to their needs and concerns.

We'll explore the importance of efficiency in content marketing and provide practical tips to help you streamline your efforts. Buckle up and let's go!

## Maximizing Impact in Content Marketing

Content marketing is all about building relationships and driving engagement, but it can easily become a time sink if not managed properly. There are so many things to supervise, manage, and control.

Efficiency in content marketing means maximizing your impact while minimizing wasted effort. Here's what it takes:

- **Targeting the Right Audience:** Spend your time crafting messages for those who are most likely to benefit from and engage with your content.
- **Optimizing Processes:** Streamline your content creation and distribution processes to save time and resources.
- **Measuring Impact:** Use data to understand what works and what doesn't. This practice allows you to focus on high-impact activities and avoid wasting time on vanity metrics.

Efficiency helps beyond letting you do more in less time. It also ensures that your content marketing efforts are driving real business results.

## Build from the Ideal Customer Profile

To be efficient with marketing planning and execution, you need to know exactly who you're targeting. A helpful tool to identify your target audience is the ICP, which we covered in Chapter 2, which is a detailed description of the type of customer who would benefit most from your product or service.

With the ICP attributes in mind, tailor your content to address the specific needs and concerns of your ideal customers.

## Align Content with Buyer Personas

Once you have your ICP, the next step is to develop detailed Buyer Personas. These personas go beyond basic demographic information and delve into the psychology of your buyers. As discussed previously, having a highly specific Buyer Persona makes your messaging more targeted, increasing its ability to land with the intended audience.

To create your Buyer Persona, research your audience first. Use surveys, interviews, and data analysis to gather insights about their preferences, behaviors, and pain points. From the information, develop the Buyer Persona profile. Include job titles, goals, challenges, and preferred content formats.

With the Buyer Persona, you can start generating specific content ideas that appeal to them. (Refer to the bonuses section on **growth forum.io/bonuses** for an example.) Some types of content are:

- **Educational Blog Posts:** Write about industry trends, common challenges, and solutions.
- **Case Studies:** Through these studies, you can showcase success stories from customers in similar roles or industries.
- **How-to Guides:** Provide step-by-step instructions on using your product or service effectively.

- **Webinars:** You can host live sessions on relevant topics that offer immediate value to your audience.
- **Infographics:** With engaging and well-designed infographics, you can share visual content that simplifies complex information.

Aligning your content with the specific needs and preferences of your Buyer Personas can create more effective marketing materials.

## Give, Nurture, Educate

By focusing on giving in a way that makes the receiver *understand*, we can nurture and educate buyers.

If we ask instead of give, we can lose our path to becoming a trusted advisor.

There is an art to giving in such a way that the receiver *understands* that you truly are giving, not asking.

When we give, we are also nurturing. As we give, we become not only more likable but also trustworthy because of the continuous value we are helping to create.

Further, a focus on education ensures that we are empowering our buyers.

Whether using a webinar, blog post, white paper, e-book, or email to deliver the content, do so with giving, nurturing, and educating top of mind because it's the purpose of that content.

## Reducing Cognitive Load

Reducing cognitive load is crucial for making it easier for your audience to engage with your content. The easier your audience can understand your content, the more efficiently you can relay your messaging.

### Simplify Your Messaging

Use clear, succinct language and avoid jargon. Break down complex concepts into easily digestible pieces. The caveat is don't be too informal. B2B transactions can take on a casual tone, but if it comes across as though you're talking to a grade-schooler, that might be too far. Maintain professionalism.

### Organize Content Logically

Our brains love it when things have patterns and flow, so make sure to structure your content in a way that flows naturally, using headings, subheadings, bullet points, and numbered lists. This tip doesn't just apply to written work. The content in infographics and webinars needs to be well organized. Avoid tangents. Stick to the main point and details that support it.

### Use Visuals

Huge blocks of text are intimidating and, let's face it, boring.

Integrate images, infographics, and videos to break up text and illustrate key points. (The next image is coming up again in a few pages!) Visuals also help with branding, especially when you keep logos, colorways, and themes consistent.

Cohesive branding aids in efficiency. It helps you make lasting impressions on your customers, who will immediately associate certain visual cues with your company.

### Provide Summaries

Include summaries at the beginning or end of your content to highlight the main takeaways. As we said above, bullet points are great because readers can find and read the main points.

### Interactive Content

This step will take more effort, but it's worth it to increase engagement. Create quizzes, calculators, and other interactive tools for people to use. Such features make information more memorable.

## Additional Tips for Content Efficiency

Here are other tips we've learned throughout the years:

- **Repurpose Content:** Maximize the value of your content by repurposing it across different formats and channels. For example, you can turn one blog post into a video, an infographic, and a social media post.
- **Automate Where Possible:** Use automation tools to streamline repetitive tasks such as email marketing, social media posting, and lead nurturing.
- **Outsource When Necessary:** Don't be afraid to outsource tasks that are outside your expertise or that consume too much time. Freelancers and agencies can help with content creation, graphic design, and more. (Getting each piece of the system in place means the entire process works better.)
- **Collaborate With Your Team:** Unfortunately, some companies only see their employees as job descriptions. If that's you, you may be missing out. Some of your employees likely have skills and knowledge in areas outside of their assigned roles. You can leverage these strengths to improve efficiency in digital marketing. You won't have to outsource since you already have team members that can address your current needs. Collaborative tools like Trello, Asana, and Slack can help you reach out and keep everyone on the same page.

- **Use Data Analytics:** Regularly analyze your content's performance to understand what resonates with your audience. Use these insights to refine your content strategy.

## Wrapping Up:
## How To Create Efficient Content

Efficiency in content marketing isn't just about doing more with less—it's about doing the right things better.

The goal is to produce content that engages your audience and drives meaningful business results through giving, nurturing, and education.

## BUYER ENABLEMENT BEGINS WITH EMPATHY

"The alternative to the Golden Rule is much more productive. I call it the Platinum Rule: 'Treat others the way they want to be treated.' Ah hah! What a difference. The Platinum Rule accommodates the feelings of others. The focus of relationships shifts from 'This is what I want, so I'll give everyone the same thing' to 'Let me first understand what they want, and then I'll give it to them.'"

—TONY ALESSANDRA

If sales is a game about change, and if it is necessary to understand where in the Five Stages of Awareness each buyer is, how can we get started on that?

*What buyer enablement really aims to do is this: help buyers embrace the most common path through their complex buying process.*

Within the V.I.S.I.O.N. Selling Methodology and the deal mechanics laid out in the previous chapter, for us, empathy needs to be deployed during Discovery. This is where we need to sense-check and truly learn what internal blockers may exist. Because it's rare that you as a seller are competing with other products or service offerings, but **it's very common to be competing against internal priorities, budgets, and people.** A great question to ask is, "Where is this project in the priority right now?"

A step back to discuss how to understand another person's perspective…

It begins with asking questions and listening. Carl Rogers, in *Becoming a Person*, discusses the importance of listening holistically. How do you truly understand the other person? He writes, "Is it necessary to permit oneself to understand another? I think it is. Our first reaction to most of the statements (which we hear from other people) is an evaluation or judgment, rather than an understanding of it…Very rarely do we permit ourselves to *understand* precisely what the meaning of the statement is to the other person."

Instead of saying, "That can't be right" or "That's reasonable," we *can* wait to fully comprehend and also ask questions to get to clarity.

The importance of active listening cannot be emphasized enough. Combine active listening with these behaviors:

- Be attentive
- Ask open-ended questions
- Ask probing questions
- Request clarification
- Paraphrase
- Be attuned to and reflect feelings
- Summarize

Empathizing with the buyer's problems is a safe starting point. Do you know what priorities your buyer has at the moment?

What trends or themes are they seeing in their business?

What is changing in their marketplace?

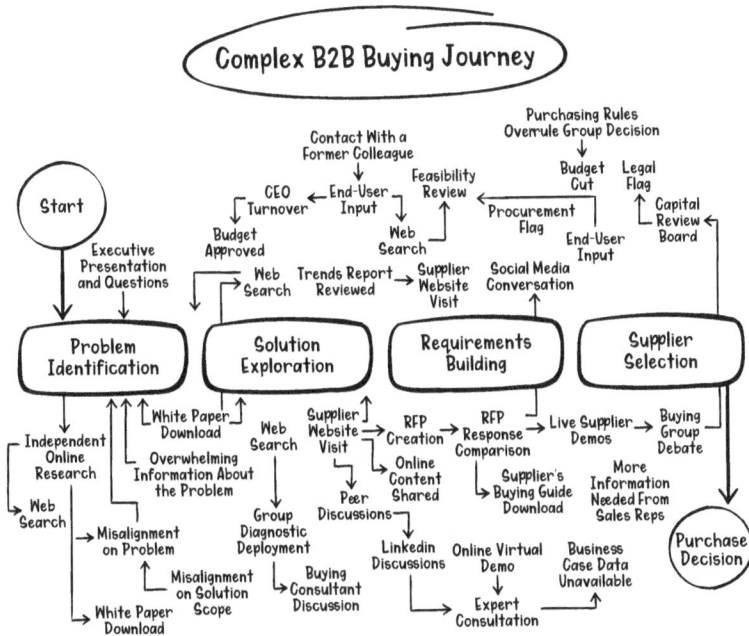

Complex B2B Buying Journey

For emphasis we again provide the Gartner-inspired buyer journey above. How can we know for sure that we are truly understanding our buyers?

Rand Fishkin, one of our podcast guests, said on the show that if you use the same language that your best customers use to describe their problem and your solution, you'll see the results. (*Direct access to this episode can be found at growthforum.io/bonuses*).

Here are a few questions to ponder.

**Ask yourself:**

- What DiSC profile am I working with? (To be unpacked soon.)

- Where is the buyer in their buying journey?
- What does the buyer NEED to know right now?
- What reservations have they expressed so far?
- Do I truly understand those?
- Is it possible the buyer is drawing their conclusions on areas we haven't yet addressed? (If we aren't answering, they will be.)
- What is the most common *valuable* path based on the experience of the seller?

**It's not:**

- Putting together a big presentation that makes it too hard for buyers to gain awareness, get clarity toward change, and gain consensus with the committee
- Skipping steps in the process just because the buyer seems ready to go right now
- Going too fast or too slow—the pacing of the overall deal and the rhythm of sales activity matters

## HOW TO POSITION HOLISTICALLY (AS A GUIDE)

To show you understand the buyer, position yourself as a guide.

How can you offer value where they are right now? Think back to the thought process we used when mapping out the sales stages to align with the buyer information gap.

Here's how that might sound...

- These are the things we want you to think about.
- These are some of the challenges.
- These are some steps to take before making a decision.
- Business case validation: this is what it would mean if you go forward.

To give an example, in selling P3 Recovery, we've added a step where we ask buyers if their lawyer has had experience with franchise deals. If yes, they get a specific next step. If not, they will get a separate next step that first educates that lawyer about the details of franchise deals so the lawyer can properly and efficiently play their role.

When setting oneself up as a guide, from the beginning of the process, this kind of question and value-add is expected and appreciated.

### The Polite Walk Away

Sometimes, it just isn't time for the buyer and their committee.

Ask: Is it true that this project isn't in the top three right now? (Or your version of this.)

Sometimes, this deflates the tension in one of two ways.

First, it might be that it is a priority, and this question creates energy and drive.

Second, it might not be the right time. Then, say, "Why don't we pause for two or three months and really get our roadmap nailed down? (You can also work on the business case and implementation plan here.) Then we can come back and get started when we are all ready. How's that sound?"

## MIRRORING COMMUNICATION STYLES FOR BETTER CONVERSATIONS

Before moving on, though, we want to flip it all on its head a bit… because what might matter more than anything as far as communication styles goes is how well you *mirror* your buying counterpart.

**Mirroring is how well you can match styles.**

Matching styles creates comfort and a feeling of being in tune with one another, which can be a strong determinant of how well conversations feel and actually progress. There are limits to this, of course, so part of it is trying it out and seeing what experience teaches you.

Likeability and feeling comfortable are useful but only to the extent that you, as the seller, continue providing the value necessary to fill information gaps at each stage.

In order to mirror, let's unpack DiSC further.

### Dancing with the DiSC

The DiSC assessment can be clarified into four quadrants.

**Dominant:** A style which has direct and guarded behaviors, prefers faster-paced, task-oriented discussions and actions.

**Influence:** Usually has direct and open behaviors, wants faster-paced, people-oriented discussions and actions.

**Steadiness:** Typically has indirect and open behaviors, wants slower-paced people-oriented discussions and actions.

**Conscientious:** Where one has indirect and guarded behaviors, wants slower-paced task-oriented discussions and actions.

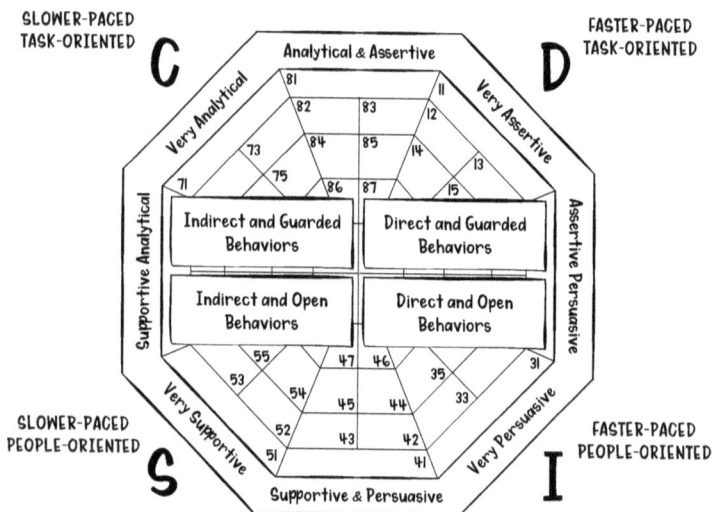

Is it a good idea to learn how to use each style?

Yes!

This will help you in situations where your buyers have a different style from your preferred one.

When working with a Dominant buyer:

- Be clear, specific, brief, and organized with an agenda
- Stick to business
- Don't force a personal relationship

When working with an Influencing buyer:

- Give them a spot in the limelight
- Create an atmosphere of excitement, fun, and variety

With a Steady buyer:

- Give them opportunities to contribute to the discussion
- Be patient
- Respond to their questions and concerns

And with a Conscientious buyer:

- Be prompt, prepared, and precise
- Allow them time to think
- Be comfortable with silences

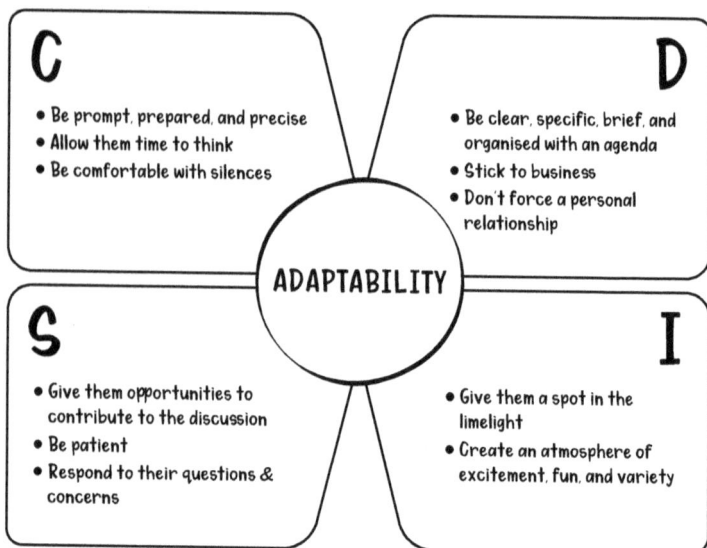

**C**
- Be prompt, prepared, and precise
- Allow them time to think
- Be comfortable with silences

**D**
- Be clear, specific, brief, and organised with an agenda
- Stick to business
- Don't force a personal relationship

**ADAPTABILITY**

**S**
- Give them opportunities to contribute to the discussion
- Be patient
- Respond to their questions & concerns

**I**
- Give them a spot in the limelight
- Create an atmosphere of excitement, fun, and variety

In fact, adapting your style is crucial to making every buyer feel comfortable speaking with you while demonstrating your competency and desire to add value to their buyer's journey.

If you're not clear on someone's style, a good default is to show that you are always prepared, are ready to provide value and ask questions, and, of course, are eager to listen to their point of view.

### Basics of Rapport Building

Likeability is a good first step in a relationship. The fact is, though, that not everyone will like you. But even without likeability, rapport can be built.

To build rapport, make the buyer the hero of the story. Always adjust and adapt to the buyer's needs, which requires *listening*, just like Lui did in the News Corp story featured in the Bonus Chapter.

Apply the platinum rule, within reason—we still want to share our insights, especially if the buyer is pre-awareness. (*The Challenger*

*Sale* method is valid and focuses on bringing unexpected value to the forefront of conversations.)

Four elements help us to do this:

**Empathy:** Understand other people's perspectives (beyond your own point of view)

Do this through active listening and reflective responses, by expressing genuine care and concern, and by offering support. Only 7% of communication is what you say.

**Energy:** Be present

Do this through mirroring, matching body language, and showing empathy. Diarize mental tasks with your phone on "Do Not Disturb." 55% of communication is nonverbal.

**Body Language & Facial Expressions:** Engage with the buyer

Again, mirroring will reduce relationship tension, and people will more readily open up to you; also, establishing a connection creates a sense of familiarity, subconscious comfort, and a feeling of being understood and accepted.

If the buyer's body language is closed, try slowing down, asking questions, and truly tuning into them, all while using an open posture, eye contact, leaning in, and facial expressions.

**Intonation:** How the voice rises and falls

38% of communication is tone. Matching tone and quality of who you are communicating with allows for greater emotional attunement, which can create a deeper sense of connection. Someone who sounds like they are on the same emotional wavelength is more trustworthy; similar intonation patterns can make the conversation flow more smoothly.

Rapport is useful, but even the best rapport is unlikely to progress a deal to a productive conclusion.

Rapport is a great start, but it doesn't build trust. Trust comes from adding value.

That's where the commercial ROI comes in…

## INTRO TO THE BUSINESS CASE FRAMEWORK

Some people just know that they want to go a certain way. Whether they are intuitive decision-makers or can extrapolate effectively from a small amount of data, it smells right.

Even these people will likely have someone on their team who wants to see the business case laid out.

Can you be the one to cocreate and develop this with them?

If you are, then the endorsement you receive from this champion internally will lead to better discussions on that business case as it gets amended and moves through the approval process within the Buying Committee.

It's really about being part of the conversation from the beginning. That's much more comforting than being a seller who interrupts a conversation midway.

So what are some ways to be at the forefront of these conversations? Well, it's about an outreach strategy that provides value through outbound. We will get to this in later chapters.

But when we do get there, it will be critical to have done some homework. Without a background in basic business principles, you will be unequipped to have such discussions productively.

### The Implementation Plan

Often, the biggest question buyers ask themselves is not "How will we pay for this?" or "Will this actually have an ROI?" but instead **"Can we actually implement this?"**

Will you let your buyers imagine how to do this themselves, leaving them with unanswered questions? Or will you be their intentional guide, facilitating the steps along the roadmap that you cocreate?

You are the seller who has sold and implemented the complex B2B sale for many clients. Be the guide.

## PRAGMATIC RESEARCH

With information a tap or click away, it's critical to take a few moments —that's really all it takes—to learn the basics about your prospects.

What not to do: do an internet search from the car moments before your face-to-face meeting. Yes, I experienced this with a salesperson I was shadowing.

Instead, develop a process that helps you learn their basic business history, what they're up to, and what they are hoping to do. Past, present, and future.

In Chapter 2: Finding Your Target, we already outlined the steps to creating your ICP and Buyer Persona.

Remember, it can be awkward to share these facts to show off what you know about someone's personal history. Quoting someone's LinkedIn profile directly versus saying, "I love what you're sharing about XYZ on LinkedIn" generally has two different effects.

People like to know that you are prepared but don't appreciate being scrutinized, because it feels weird. Revealing you know a plethora of personal facts is a quick way to develop relationship tension. Instead, there are better ways to prepare oneself.

# USING A P&L TO UNDERSTAND A BUYER'S BUSINESS

Part of your pragmatic research will be to use a profit and loss (P&L) statement to get to know your client's world from the business perspective.

This work is particularly helpful when changing roles or taking on accounts in a different vertical within your company. Even if you're seasoned, updating your understanding of how businesses in your industry are operating is helpful to keep your discussions relevant. (When we get to the cold-calling segment in Chapter 6: Earning the Right, you might be surprised at how many C-level executives say that sellers who cold call them are not prepared.)

A P&L statement, or income statement, provides a summary of a company's revenues, costs, and expenses over a period of time, revealing the company's ability to generate profit by increasing revenue, reducing costs, or both. Salespeople can use insights from a P&L statement to tailor their sales strategies in several ways:

1. **Identifying Budget Priorities and Constraints:**
   By reviewing how revenues are generated and where the most significant expenses lie, salespeople can identify what aspects of their product or service may be most appealing. For instance, if a buyer's largest expense is labor, solutions that promise efficiency and reduce labor costs might be particularly attractive.

2. **Tailoring the Value Proposition:** Understanding the buyer's major sources of revenue and cost centers allows the salesperson to craft messages that resonate deeply. If the P&L shows high marketing expenses but revenue growth is stagnant, a salesperson can highlight how their product or service might increase market penetration or improve marketing ROI.

3. **Timing the Sale:** Seasonal trends in revenue can inform when a buyer might be more open to making purchasing decisions. For example, a business might be more willing to invest in new initiatives during a peak revenue period.

4. **Strategic Discussions with Buyers:** Salespeople armed with knowledge about the buyer's financials can engage in more meaningful and strategic discussions with decision-makers. This establishes the salesperson not just as a vendor but as a valuable consultant who understands the financial impact of their offerings.

By effectively interpreting a P&L statement, you can position yourself as a strategic partner who understands the economic realities your buyers face. This not only helps in aligning the product or service with the buyer's needs but also in building a baseline level of trust and credibility.

You *should* have done your research and should avoid coming to a meeting unprepared. Unless you don't want the deal, of course!

## INTRO TO OBJECTIONS (AND STALLS)

| Stall | Terms/Conditions | True Objection |

If you pick up the phone for a cold call and the person answering says, "I'm not interested," that is not an objection. That is a stall.

How can they not be interested if they haven't even listened to the insight you have to share with them? Let alone what problems you might be able to solve alongside them later on…

That's why this is a stall, not an objection. It's someone's way of saying, "I don't have time for this right now." They will say anything not to have this conversation right now.

What we will see later, in Chapter 9, is a discussion about true objections.

**The definition of an objection is a request for more information before moving forward.**

Being able to notice these and properly ask follow-up questions is the difference between losing deals as they move toward closing and smoothly wrapping up those same deals and marking them as closed/won.

## EMOTIONAL AND PSYCHOLOGICAL SAFETY FOR BUYERS: REDUCING ANXIETY AND BUILDING TRUST

Let's talk about something often swept under the rug in B2B marketing: the emotional and psychological safety of your buyers. You know, those real, live human beings making the decision to buy your product or service. They're not just numbers in your CRM or targets for your next campaign. They're people with real anxieties, doubts, and fears. If you can address these aspects, then you'll build stronger connections, foster trust, and ultimately make your buyers feel secure and confident in their decisions.

## Understanding Buyer Anxiety: What's Keeping Them Up at Night?

Buyer enablement is about empowering your buyers with the knowledge, tools, and support they need to make informed purchasing decisions confidently. But they can't if they have doubts and fears about the offer, the transaction, or the implementation. You need to address these issues to give your clients peace of mind and assurance.

Before you can address buyer anxiety, you need to understand it. Buying, especially in a B2B context, is a big deal. There's a lot on the line—money, reputation, and career advancement. One small mistake can destroy years of effort on the buyer's end. Here's what might be running through your buyers' minds.

- **Fear of Making the Wrong Decision:** "What if this solution doesn't work?"
- **Budget Concerns:** "Is this the best use of our funds?"
- **Job Security:** "Will my boss think I made the right choice?"
- **Complexity of Implementation:** "How hard will this be to integrate?"

Recognize these concerns and you're already a step ahead. Your goal is to minimize these anxieties through empathy, active listening, and genuine support. It won't just take a few words of encouragement —this isn't some feel-good movie. You'll need to make an effort in your process to improve the results.

## Empathy: Walk a Mile in Their Shoes

Empathy isn't just a buzzword. It's the cornerstone of building trust. When buyers feel understood, their anxiety diminishes. Here's how you can infuse empathy into your sales process.

### Practice Active Listening

Don't just wait for your turn to speak. Really listen to what your buyers are saying. Reflect on what you've heard to show understanding.

For example, you can say something like, "I hear that you're concerned about the integration process. Let's dive into those details and see how we can make the transition seamless for you."

There, you've already shown that you're paying attention. We'll discuss active listening even more in a bit.

### Acknowledge Their Fears

Validate their feelings instead of brushing them off. Tell them that it's okay to admit that implementing a new solution can be daunting. You can say that you understand how choosing the right software can feel overwhelming.

Show the customer that you've supported many clients through this transition and that you'll be there for them every step of the way.

### Share Relatable Stories

Use case studies and testimonials that buyers can relate to. Show them how others in similar positions have succeeded.

This practice serves as an assurance that real people have gotten good results from you.

Make sure to say something like "One of our clients in your industry had the same concerns, but here's how we helped them achieve their goals…"

## Active Listening:
## More Than Just Hearing Words

Active listening goes beyond hearing. It's about understanding the full context of your buyer's concerns. They say that they're worried about how their manager might react to this transaction, but the real reason they're saying this is because they're worried about keeping their job.

Having this level of perception allows you to dig deeper and really recognize the speaker's true feelings. Here are our tips:

- **Ask Open-Ended Questions:** Encourage buyers to share more about their needs and concerns.
- **Summarize and Clarify:** Repeat what you've heard to ensure you've understood correctly. This practice is a signal that you're present in the moment.
- **Body Language Matters:** If you're meeting in person or over video, use positive body language to show you're engaged and interested. Lean forward, mirror their actions, and smile and nod a lot.

## Prioritizing Buyer Enablement:
## Support Every Step of the Way

Buyer enablement is how you provide the support and tools your buyers need to feel confident in their decision. Here's how to prioritize it.

- **Educational Content:** Create and share resources that help buyers understand your product and how it will benefit them.
- **Personalized Support:** We recommend tailoring your approach to meet the unique needs of each buyer. Provide personalized consultations and dedicated

support channels when possible. It's how you can make them feel like they're your priority.

- **Transparent Communication:** Be open and honest about what your product can and cannot do. Set realistic expectations from the start.
- **Post-Sale Support:** Your relationship with the buyer doesn't end once you've sold the product. Ensure they have the support they need to succeed with your product. This is how you gain loyalty and even word-of-mouth marketing, improving your reputation as a seller.

## Building Trust: The Foundation of a Secure Buyer

Trust is the bedrock of any successful buyer-seller relationship—any relationship, really. Without it, even the best product, business, or deal can fail to gain traction.

- **Consistency Is Key:** Be consistent in your messaging, actions, and follow-ups. Reliability breeds trust.
- **Honesty Over Hype:** Avoid exaggerating the benefits of your product—that's how you start with a bang and end with a whimper. Instead, focus on honest, clear communication.
- **Showcase Expertise:** Demonstrate your knowledge and expertise in your industry. You should be able to provide valuable insights that help your buyers.
- **Build a Human Connection:** People buy from people. Build rapport by showing genuine interest in your buyers as individuals, not mere clients who will increase your numbers. Heck, ask them about their hobbies. If you're creative enough, you can steer the conversation from their love of say, Pokémon, to the product you're selling.

## Practical Tips to Reduce Buyer Anxiety

Here are other ways you can reduce the fears and hesitant attitudes of your target buyers:

- **Simplify the Buying Process:** Make it as easy as possible for buyers to understand and engage with your sales process.
  - → Example: Use clear, jargon-free language and provide step-by-step guides.
- **Offer Free Trials or Demos:** Let buyers experience your product firsthand without any pressure.
  - → Example: "We offer a free 30-day trial so you can see how our solution works for you."
- **Provide Clear ROI Metrics:** Show buyers the potential return on investment they can expect from your product.
  - → Example: "Our clients typically see a 20% increase in efficiency within the first three months."
- **Create a Safe Space for Feedback:** Encourage buyers to share their thoughts and concerns without fear of judgment.
  - → Example: "We value your feedback and want to ensure our solution meets your needs. What concerns do you have?"
- **Be Accessible:** Ensure buyers can easily reach you with questions or concerns. Give your email, phone, or any other available point of contact.
  - → Example: "You can reach us via phone, email, or live chat. We're here to help!"

## Making Emotional and Psychological Safety a Priority

In the fast-paced world of B2B marketing, it's easy to forget that your buyers are more than just leads. They're people with real emotions and concerns. By prioritizing emotional and psychological safety, the sale gets closed, yes, but also a lasting relationship based on trust and mutual respect kicks off.

Remember, empathy, active listening, and buyer enablement are not merely strategies; they're manifestations of your commitment to understanding and supporting your buyers. When you make your buyers feel heard, valued, and secure, you reduce their anxiety and pave the way for a successful, long-term partnership.

So go ahead, make that connection, and watch how it transforms your buyer relationships.

Now, we want you to take a step back and reflect on how you're approaching buyers' fears and what you can now include in your strategy. Good luck and have fun!

## SOUND BYTE SUMMARY

— It's the buyer that will take the leap of faith, despite their fear—help them get what they need so they are as ready as possible when they decide to jump.

— Buyers don't buy the products or feature sets you're selling, they buy the outcome you're helping them to achieve— engage with insight and then continue giving, nurturing, and educating to provide all information necessary to progress.

— It's A-okay to be passionate about your products and services, you might even love what you're doing—we do! —and yet we need to be careful about ensuring the commercial ROI is built out with the buyer.

— The business case, if developed alongside buyers, will help them get to a point of decision. (More on this in Chapter 8: The Buying Committee.)

To get access to all of the templates, frameworks, tools, and podcast episodes referenced in this book, visit this link: **growthforum.io/bonuses**

## NEXT UP

Now that we've understood why to focus on enabling buyers using empathy and value-driven communication within their buying journey, it's time to enter the pursuit by making a sales plan and developing the operating rhythm of your sales cadence.

# CHAPTER 5

# ENTERING THE PURSUIT

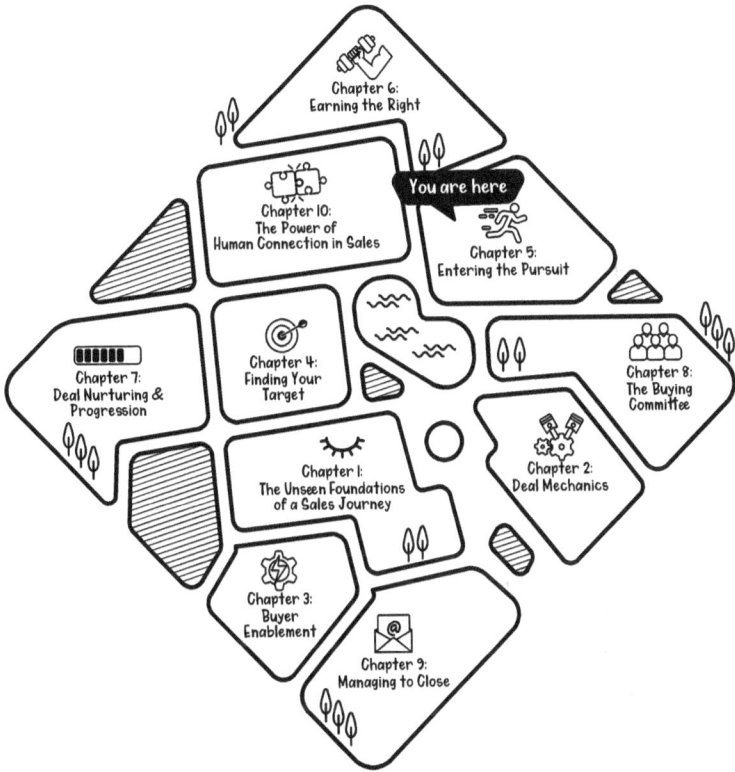

Chapter 6:
Earning the Right

Chapter 10:
The Power of
Human Connection in Sales

You are here

Chapter 5:
Entering the Pursuit

Chapter 7:
Deal Nurturing &
Progression

Chapter 4:
Finding Your
Target

Chapter 8:
The Buying
Committee

Chapter 1:
The Unseen Foundations
of a Sales Journey

Chapter 2:
Deal Mechanics

Chapter 3:
Buyer
Enablement

Chapter 9:
Managing to Close

## How to *enter the pursuit* of buyers, beginning with a sales plan.

Marc Marano pounded the pavement when he went to America to sell franchises for his fitness brand, F45. He was able to sell loads of franchises and help people see the future vision of what was possible. And he did it in a unique way to find a needle in a haystack, in a market so big with existing players like Orangetheory Fitness, LA Fitness, and others, but he was able to create something out of nothing.

If Marc had Lusha and some of the tools available today, he might have sold double what he did. The strategy for sellers today is how to adopt modern technology to make it work for you.

Many don't have the perseverance and the resilience that Marc does, who is someone who will keep going until he succeeds. He truly has the essence of mindset that we described in the opening chapter. He doesn't have a limit of what's possible. This is where sellers *need* to follow Marc's lead. You can enter with a scarcity mindset or an abundance mindset: the choice is yours.

Most people fail *before* the pursuit begins.

That key decision happens before carefully laying out a strategy to engage their list, prospect, and grow deal flow through discovery.

Chapter 5 is technically going to be about setting up your prospecting strategy, while Chapter 6: Earning the Right, is the beginning of implementing your strategy with regards to prospecting, discovery, and deal nurturing.

To begin, let's focus on the sales plan before going into who to focus on and the seven pillars of a great cadence.

# BUILD YOUR SALES PLAN

"If you fail to plan, you're planning to fail."

—BENJAMIN FRANKLIN

Ninety percent of founders, business leaders, and salespeople don't use a sales plan, which is surprising because everyone knows hope alone is not a strategy.

Imagine you're about to go into the world's tallest building. About to get into the elevator, you see a sign that says, "This building was not designed to specification. It was designed by an award-winning architect. They've built buildings before, so they didn't use any plans but instead built the building based on their previous knowledge."

Having read the sign and knowing the risk, what would you do?

Would you still get in the elevator and hit the top floor button?

Or would you quickly make your way to the exit?

You might be thinking, *What does this have to do with me, with sales?*

Because there's a risk that many salespeople are accepting—are *choosing*—when deciding *not* to use a sales plan.

Using a sales plan is controlling what you can control. And being accountable to that plan.

Without one, the strategy is hope.

The reality is, according to Salesintel, 65% of salespeople are missing their target.

Yes, the market is difficult. But when we've worked with top performers in a number of industries and roles, we see that they use a sales plan to understand their daily activities and stick to it.

If you hear a sales guru say it's not about planning, feel free to tell them, calmly and respectfully of course, that you now subscribe to a different philosophy!

# Sales Plan Introduction

How can you get a snapshot of whether your sales activities and sales pipeline are setting you up to meet your quota on time, or even blow past it?

The simplest way is through a sales planning exercise.

**Step 1:** Input how long you have to achieve your target.

**Step 2:** Enter the metrics that will enable you to achieve your target.

**Step 3:** Review the metrics and then move them to the sales plan.

**Step 4:** Understand how many target accounts must be added to your list.

## SALES PLANNING CALCULATOR

Step 1. Enter the working weeks available for you to achieve your target

| HOW LONG DO YOU HAVE TO ACHIEVE YOUR TARGET? | MONTHS | WEEKS |
|---|---|---|
| Working weeks in a year | 11 | 48 |

Step 2. Enter the metrics that will enable you to achieve your target

| HOW LONG DO YOU HAVE TO ACHIEVE YOUR TARGET? | | VALUE |
|---|---|---|
| Sales Target | $ | 1,000,000 |
| Average Deal Size | $ | 7,000 |
| Out of 100 - How many proposals/quotes convert to closed-won (%)? | | 50% |
| Out of 100 - How many discovery calls turn into a proposal or quote? | | 60% |
| Out of 100 - How many people book a meeting from an Omni Channel Outreach sequence? | | 50% |
| Average Sequences Executed Per Hour | | 10 |

Step 3. Review the sales metrics and then move these metrics to your Sales Plan

| SALES PERFORMANCE METRICS | PER ANNUM | PER MONTH | PER WEEK |
|---|---|---|---|
| Opportunities won | 143 | 13 | 3 |
| Proposals sent | 286 | 26 | 6 |
| Discovery meetings | 477 | 43 | 10 |
| Conversations | 954 | 86 | 20 |
| 1-hour time-blocks scheduled | 95 | 9 | 2 |
| Prospects | 1,908 | 172 | 40 |

Step 4. Review how many target accounts need to be added to your list.

| PROSPECT LIST BUILDING ACTIVITY | PER ANNUM | PER MONTH | PER WEEK |
|---|---|---|---|
| Target prospects required for outreach | 1,908 | 172 | 40 |

*Note: This sales calculator is in your bonus resources vault found here:*
*https://growthforum.io/bonuses*

For immediate results, get started right now. You might be surprised at how taking just a few moments at the 30,000-foot view will allow you to relax and gain confidence in the simple steps and activities needed today to reach your targets by the end of the year.

We highly recommend using your sales plan so you aren't one of the 90% not using one, but also because it will let you see the big picture and then break it down into manageable steps from there.

If you find a way to simplify this calculator, or modify it to your needs, let us know in the Growth Forum community over at growthforum.io.

## The Dynamics of Appointments

When the decision is made to put something on your calendar, it has gone through a filter of priority and importance. By definition, not everything even gets onto the calendar, and not everything gets circled as very important.

As an aside, consider the logic or protocol you are currently using to decide whether something goes on the calendar at all. This might help you respond to incoming requests, especially if you have a calendar or booking system that allows prospects to book appointments with you.

The appointment itself works psychologically because it is a scarce event—it happens at a specific time and place—that will demand your preparation and focus.

Before getting off the meeting, remember to ask: "What do you want to happen after this meeting?"

This sets things in motion for the next one.

# WHO TO TRULY FOCUS ON—KEY ACCOUNT PLANNING

An **account planning document** is a strategic tool used in **B2B sales** to help you win and retain your most valuable customers. Now, the reason we include this here is because you might be re-engaging a previous or existing customer to continue a service that is going to lapse or to try a new version of a product or service. If a buyer enjoyed working with you before and they still fit the ICP, then they might just be an example of a key account, as well as one to include on the prospect list.

Let's dive into the details.

## What Is Key Account Planning?

- Key account planning is an **account-based sales strategy** focusing on your most valuable customers. These key accounts typically make up about 20% of your customer base but drive around 80% of your business revenue.
- Instead of treating all customers equally, key account planning tailors efforts to these high-value customers' unique needs and decision-making factors.
- The goal is to create a plan that nurtures a larger, mutually beneficial relationship over time.

## Key Account Management:

- Key account planning and key account management (KAM) go hand-in-hand.
- KAM involves implementing the activities identified in your key account plans.
- It includes dedicating resources (such as account managers and sales reps) and using the right tools to keep and grow business with key customers.

- Key account managers build meaningful relationships beyond the initial sale, aiming to increase revenue and returns.

### Benefits of Successful Key Account Planning:

- **Increased Revenue:** By strategically tailoring engagement approaches, account planning helps generate more revenue faster.
- **Reduced Customer Churn:** Retaining existing key accounts is more cost-effective than acquiring new ones.
- **Improved Sales Efficiency:** Efficient sales teams can close more deals using fewer resources.

Account planning enables B2B companies to prioritize opportunities, uncover expansion potential, and build long-term, trusted relationships with their most valuable customers.

You can establish trust, nurture relationships, and drive revenue growth by creating effective account plans.

## SEVEN PILLARS OF A GREAT CADENCE

During a workshop for AirPlus in Germany with approximately 50 salespeople, the topic of **cadence** came up. (Cadences are structured plans of communication and outreach tasks you make to a prospect or lead over a period of time.)

We discussed using SMS (text messaging) as part of the cadence.

Initially, many in the room were reluctant about using SMS. But Paolo decided to embrace the cadence and went on to execute all elements of the cadence.

What transpired? Net new meetings. From those net new meetings, more qualified opportunities. And the rest is history. He became a top hunter (a term for those winning net new business) globally.

Cadence matters.

It matters because there is a rhythm to learning, a process of change, and a natural cycle for buyers.

So cadence matters. It doesn't matter what type of campaign it is —whether inbound or outbound.

You need to ensure you have the right process for follow-up.

Here are some interesting statistics: 80% of inbound leads engage between the 9th and 13th touch points.

Yet most sales teams give up after just two attempts.

The data shows that many of the leads interact after the third outreach cluster. (We have a case study to share in just a short bit.)

Now, we are not saying you need to follow this exact structure. The best structure is the one you test and define is right for your lead profile.

Let's start by laying out the elements of a successful sales cadence.

**Target**—Developing the right target list to prospect into

**Touches**—Total number of touches

**Interval**—The time between each activity

**Channels**—The different channels or communication methods that will be used

**Content**—The message you deliver with each touch point

**Duration**—The time between the first activity and the last activity

**Cycle**—Rest period and number of times you will execute your cadence

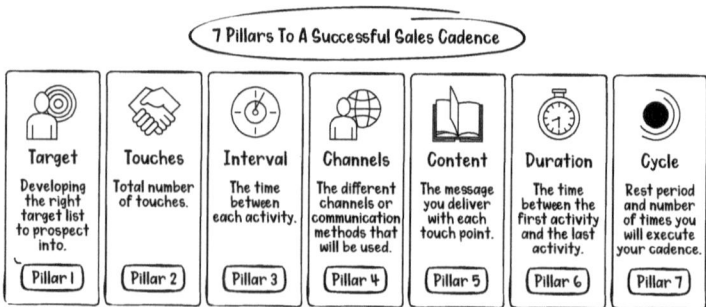

7 Pillars To A Successful Sales Cadence

| Target | Touches | Interval | Channels | Content | Duration | Cycle |
|---|---|---|---|---|---|---|
| Developing the right target list to prospect into. | Total number of touches. | The time between each activity. | The different channels or communication methods that will be used. | The message you deliver with each touch point. | The time between the first activity and the last activity. | Rest period and number of times you will execute your cadence. |
| Pillar 1 | Pillar 2 | Pillar 3 | Pillar 4 | Pillar 5 | Pillar 6 | Pillar 7 |

Let's break these down a bit.

We've already discussed **Target** in Chapter 4: Finding Your Target, where you developed your ICP and corresponding Buyer Personas.

**Touches** is next. Many buyers will not engage until somewhere between 9–13 touches. Some longer. Use a cluster of messages within a short period of time across multiple channels.

With **Interval**, first consider that you might touch on multiple channels with a similar message in bunches. We suggest touching multiple channels, such as voicemail, text, and email, to give yourself a chance to reach the buyer in at least one method. Then, put some time between this and the next series of touches.

**Channels** can be phone, text, email, social platforms, face to face, and so on. Our approach tends to be phone-led with an aim to get the buyer connected with us quickly. *Then make email the hero.* (More coming up on how to craft great emails in Chapter 6: Earning the Right.)

## Multi-Channel Strategy

|        | Monday | Tuesday | Wednesday | Thursday | Friday |
|--------|--------|---------|-----------|----------|--------|
| Week 1 | 📞🗨✉in |         |           |          | 📞🗨✉💬 |
| Week 2 |        |         | 🗨✉▶💬     |          |        |
| Week 3 |        |         | 🗨✉💬      |          |        |

**Content** is all about delivering the right message for a particular buyer at the right time in their buying journey. Content can be written, an image, or even a video. It doesn't have to be your own content. Sharing content from a source or company you know your buyer respects is completely fine and saves time from you always needing to create or remix your own. Even mixing in GIFs is worthwhile. The famous Millhouse frisbee toss GIF was used to get the attention of a Chief Financial Officer (CFO) from a $200M business for us.

**Duration** will depend on how long the sales cycle typically takes. Start with benchmarks for what you are selling and check that against the buying cycle time you are hearing from buyers. You might decide to mirror that duration.

**Cycle** refers to how long a rest period should be before re-engaging a prospect. Yes, you will be putting the prospect back through your same cadence again! (Maybe by then you will have made a few tweaks.) Just because this prospect was a "No" the first time doesn't mean they won't be ready the next.

---

### Checkpoint 5: Content Calendars

*Just as there are checkpoints in a sales and buying journey, there will be checkpoints through this book to test your learning and application: learning without application is simply entertainment.*

#### Enabling Content Marketing (and Sales Touches) at Scale for Better Relationships

*It's easy to put off a simple content calendar. Maybe you want to personalize, and you feel that a content calendar (attached to a cadence) feels too mechanized. With the appropriate care, it isn't. In fact, those detailed, timely touches can be a differentiator in making you stand out from the sea of sameness. Invest in a multichannel strategy with a simple cadence creation exercise, then mount that onto a content calendar for your key leads.*

---

## Outbound vs. Inbound Case Study:
## P3 Recovery

Inbound has a built-in illusion—not all leads will be great leads. Inbound makes you feel good because people are coming to you. That's great, if you then go and qualify them. But unqualified leads that aren't your target, if you close them, can be a pain in the rear as customers, costing you more time and resources to serve.

Paid advertising gives a similar illusion, a false sense that it is working. For instance, with the big social media companies, *they* are in control of their system. Let's say one day your lead acquisition is $10 per lead. Then the next day it goes up to $30. That still might be okay for a few months, but it slowly cannibalizes itself.

In the previous chapter, we introduced the concept of "Return on Effort," anchored by the identification of your ICP, which is your guiding star in prospecting. The ICP focuses your efforts. Your sales activity will have clearer results when you hone in on revenue-raising activities—those critical, high-payoff actions that propel your sales forward.

Prospecting, researching, list building, cold outreach, follow-ups, discovery meetings, preparation, demonstrations, proposals, deal follow-ups, and CRM updates are the bread and butter of a sales professional's day.

These are juxtaposed against low-payoff activities like instant replies, manual tasks, administration, internal meetings, and task switching, which, while necessary, should not consume the bulk of your valuable time.

Now, P3 Recovery is a franchise model, B2B sales with emotional buyers, given it is spending one's own money (sometimes), not the company's, leading to about 3% conversion.

Part way through 2024, Luigi wanted to compare the cost-effectiveness of outbound and inbound. It's important to do both because there's a big number of buyers that aren't in the buying phase. They are in the pre-awareness stage or in between buying cycles. (For first-time franchise owners, it's likely pre-awareness.)

Here are the results:

From cold:

- 67 prospects identified
- 28 meetings

Two tools:

- Sales Navigator to create a list
- FullEnrich to enrich the list

Then called/emailed/text

- 28 meetings
- Generated seven sales-qualified opportunities (SQQs)

When costed out, including time, call blocks, and tools:

- $5,000 for seven SQOs, or $750 per lead

Meanwhile, inbound costs about $7,500 for 100 leads. Call them, do discovery, and after that, get about four applications from those 100 leads.

- $7,500 for four SQOs, or $1,875 per lead

**Cost Comparison**

| Cold | | Inbound |
|---|---|---|
| $5,000 | Total Cost | $7,500 |
| 7 | SQOs | 4 |
| $750 | Cost per Lead | $1,875 |

When costed out, including time, call blocks, and tools.

While P3 is a franchise model and the franchise sales are B2B, Luigi also decided to apply the sales operating system to attract *members* as well—here's the data for the Port Melbourne Pre-Launch.

**The Results:**

- 256 Members Acquired
- 39% Conversion (member), averaging 10 touches
- $12,735 Total Ad Spend
- 2,369 Calls Made
- $19 Cost Per Lead
- 2,360 Emails Sent
- $49 Cost to Acquire
- 3,146 Text Messages Sent

## Port Melbourne Pre-Launch Data

| | |
|---|---|
| **256** Members Acquired | **39%** Conversion |
| **$12,735** Total Ad Spend | **2369** Calls Made |
| **$19** Cost per Lead | **2360** Emails Sent |
| **$49** Cost to Acquire | **3146** Text Messages Sent |

## TEXT MESSAGE AS SOON AS POSSIBLE

It changes the relationship dynamic because it is a different medium.

According to SimpleTexting, text messages have 98% open rate, messages are read on average within three minutes, and they have a 45% response rate. That's an instant impact.

Email is still the hero, and text messages can be used to point buyers to an email you've already sent or are about to send—just like voicemails can do.

For example: "Hey, I just sent you the discovery doc."

It also helps when producing cascading commitment. Finish a meeting, book a meeting. Use text messages to say, "Thanks for taking time to meet," to show gratitude.

Notes from a discovery meeting can also be shared via text (this is also fine to send by email).

We know this works because we've gotten feedback from clients who've said they love how we phoned them *and* texted them.

As long as it's respectful.

Consider when the best times are to send for your audience and specific buyers you've already engaged with.

Texting is also great as a follow-up. "I'm conscious of the timelines you mentioned when we met. Are you free for a call today or tomorrow?"

Or "I didn't want you to think that I'd forgotten about you..."

The fact is people are in multiple group chats (they are already on their phone a *lot*) and are often dependent on their phone. This is a big reason they are likely to see your message come through—so make the most of it!

## AUTOMATION IN MARKETING AND MULTICHANNEL STRATEGIES: TOOLS FOR PROSPECTING YOUR CLIENTS

Finding new clients can often feel like an uphill battle. With so many potential leads scattered across various platforms, how can you ensure you're reaching the right people at the right time? How can you maximize effort while ensuring that you're focusing on the right things? Automation and multichannel marketing are some of the key steps you can take to ensure things don't collapse into an absolute disaster.

These powerful approaches can transform your prospecting efforts by streamlining processes and enhancing your outreach. Automation and personalization help you efficiently segment audiences, personalize messages, and schedule campaigns, ensuring that every touchpoint is timely and relevant.

Meanwhile, a multichannel approach leverages different communication platforms to guide your prospects seamlessly through their buyer's journey. How can you leverage both in your operations? This book (and Growth Forum) dives deeper into these strategies to help you get started.

## Automation and Personalization: Taking Away the Grunt Work

Here's something that many salespeople fail to follow: in the fast-paced world of marketing, it's all about working smarter, not harder.

Yes, we often hear this advice, so what does "working smarter" really entail? Well, this concept is all about letting things (or others) work for you. You don't have to handle everything—that just leads to wasted time, frustration, even burnout. Instead, you can use automation and personalization to make everything flow without sacrificing the human touch.

## The Power of Automation

Automation isn't just about setting things on autopilot and hoping for the best—it's about using smart tools to handle the repetitive tasks that eat up your day, giving you more time to focus on the big-picture strategies that drive growth.

### Segmenting Audiences

One of the first steps in any marketing strategy is understanding who your audience is. Automation tools can help you segment your audience based on various criteria, such as demographics, behavior, and past interactions. Having these categories means you can send targeted messages that resonate with specific groups, increasing the chances of engagement and conversion.

One popular program used for segmenting audiences is Hub-Spot. It offers powerful segmentation tools that allow you to create detailed lists based on almost any criteria you can think of. Plus, it integrates seamlessly with your CRM of choice, ensuring your data is always up to date.

### Personalizing Messages

Gone are the days of one-size-fits-all marketing. Today's consumers expect messages that speak directly to them. Automation tools can help you personalize your communication at scale. You can tailor emails, social media posts, and even website content based on individual user data, creating a more engaging and relevant experience for your audience.

For this personalization strategy, we recommend programs like Kit (formerly named ConvertKit). It has automation features that let you personalize emails based on user behavior, preferences, and past interactions. You can create dynamic content blocks that change depending on who's viewing them, making each email feel like it was crafted just for the recipient.

### Scheduling Campaigns

Timing is everything in marketing. With automation tools, you can schedule your campaigns to go out at the perfect moment, even while you're asleep. Scheduling ensures your messages reach your audience when they're most likely to engage, increasing your chances of success.

Find programs that allow you to schedule social media posts across multiple platforms at optimal times. Programs like Buffer have intuitive interfaces that make it easy to manage your posting schedule, so you can stay consistent without constantly being online.

### Other Areas You Can Automate

By leveraging automation, you free up valuable time that can be better spent on strategy, creativity, and relationship-building. Automation tools handle the heavy lifting so you can focus on what matters. Here are some other specific processes you can automate to make the most of your time.

- **Lead Scoring:** Automatically assign scores to leads based on their interactions with your brand. This process helps prioritize follow-ups with the most engaged prospects, ensuring your time is spent on high-potential leads.
- **Follow-Up Reminders:** You can set automated reminders to follow up with leads at specific intervals. Thanks to this practice, you can ensure that no lead falls through the cracks and maintain a consistent communication flow.
- **Data Management:** Automatically capture and organize data from various sources into a centralized system. This reduces time spent on manual data entry and ensures your information is always up to date and easily accessible.

## Multichannel Marketing Strategy: Reaching Your Audience Where They Are

In the modern marketing landscape, a one-channel approach just doesn't cut it. Your audience is spread across various platforms, and each stage of the buyer's journey requires a different touchpoint. Instead, a multichannel marketing strategy is critical. It's the secret ingredient that lets you maximize every platform available. By effectively using different communication channels, you can guide your prospects from awareness to decision-making seamlessly.

### Social Media for Awareness

Social media is where you cast the widest net. It's perfect for building brand awareness and reaching potential customers who might not yet know about your product or service. Use platforms like Facebook, Instagram, LinkedIn, and X (formerly Twitter) to share engaging content, participate in conversations, and build a community around your brand.

**Luigi P.**

Haven't been on social for almost two weeks.

Each day I didn't post, the guilt kicked in.

But just because I wasn't posting doesn't mean nothing was happening.

In fact, it was the complete opposite.

I was spending time in Sydney with the incredible Regan Barker, watching her facilitate a group of awesome partners at Grant Thornton Australia.

I was opening a new P3 location in Melbourne with Marc Marano and Paul Goldfinch.

I was spending time in Germany with Edwige Baron, Paolo Bruzzese, and the team at AirPlus International.

And then to Brisbane with another new P3 location, and back to Melbourne with the not-so-cool David Fastuca, getting to hang with the Hub Property Group Pty Ltd and Michael Hermans, watching Brei Scolaro facilitate an awesome session on DISC.

It's safe to say the last few weeks have been eventful.

Sometimes things just take priority over others, and that's okay.

Even if you don't see someone posting on LinkedIn, it doesn't mean they aren't out there doing their thing.

However, this reinforces why I need to get my social posting system in place.

So I think I will reach out to Leslie Venetz and ask her for coaching.

No matter where she is in the world, she never seems to miss a day.

For B2B sales, LinkedIn is a great platform to increase awareness among prospective clients. However, other platforms like Instagram Stories are also crucial to increase your reach. Posts on these websites can be used to showcase behind-the-scenes content, customer testimonials, and product teasers. These capabilities help humanize your brand and create a connection with your audience.

For example, consider this post from Morgan J Ingram:

My favorite LinkedIn play right now that converts at 70%.

It's called Zelda's Boomerang.

Here is how it works.

Click on your profile views.

Find someone relevant in your ICP.

Send them a message saying this:

"Hi, Bobby, saw you viewed my profile. How can I help?"

OR

"Hi, Bobby, saw you viewed my profile. Did I do something wrong?

Both of these work very well to spark a conversation in the DMs with someone.

This helped me book a Fortune 500 company last week.

Don't sleep on the profile views feature.

There is gold in them hills, and it's up to us to prospect into them.

♻ Repost this, and I'll send you the entire prospecting flow for FREE.

P.S. Please don't copy and paste the messaging and forget to change the name from Bobby...[3]

---

[3] Morgan J Ingram, post, LinkedIn, accessed December 19, 2024, https://www.linkedin .com/feed/update/urn:li:activity:7250249306534768641/.

### Emails for Consideration

Once you've caught your audience's attention, it's time to nurture those leads through email marketing. Emails are perfect for providing valuable content, product information, and personalized offers that help prospects move from consideration to intent.

One practice you can try is drip campaigns. Set up an email drip campaign to send a series of automated emails that educate your leads about your product's benefits, share case studies, and offer special promotions.

### Personal Calls or Meetings for Decision-Making

When it comes to sealing the deal, nothing beats a personal touch. Direct communication through phone calls or face-to-face meetings can address specific concerns, answer questions, and build trust. These factors are particularly important in B2B sales, where relationships often play a crucial role in decision-making.

One area you can focus on is video calls. Use tools like Zoom or Microsoft Teams to set up virtual meetings. You can have a personal conversation without the need for physical presence, making it easier to connect with prospects no matter where they are.

### Automation in Multichannel Marketing

Managing multiple channels can be overwhelming, but automation tools can make it easier. These tools help you coordinate your efforts across different platforms, ensuring a consistent and cohesive message throughout the buyer's journey.

Here are examples of areas in multichannel marketing that can benefit from automation:

- **Email Campaigns:** Automate email sequences for different stages of the buyer's journey, such as welcome emails, follow-ups, and re-engagement campaigns. Automated A/B testing can also optimize subject lines, content, and send times.

- **Social Media Scheduling:** Plan and schedule posts across multiple social media platforms in advance. Automated responses to comments and messages can maintain engagement without manual intervention.
- **Content Management:** Automate the publication of blog posts, articles, and other content on your website and social media channels. Automated RSS feeds can also push new content to subscribers instantly.
- **Lead Nurturing:** As you gain new prospects, it's important to nurture them for easier conversion. Set up automated workflows to nurture leads through personalized content and communications based on their interactions and behaviors. This strategy is good for sending targeted emails, reminders, and follow-up messages.

## Wrapping Up:
## Automation and Multichannel Marketing in B2B Sales

Harnessing automation and multichannel marketing strategies is essential in today's B2B sales landscape. Automation optimizes time by streamlining tasks like email campaigns, social media scheduling, and lead nurturing. It's how you ensure efficiency without sacrificing personalization.

On the other hand, a robust multichannel approach ensures consistent and targeted engagement across various platforms. You have a means to guide prospects seamlessly through their buyer's journey. Together, these strategies empower sales teams to work smarter, not harder, fostering stronger relationships and driving better results. Embrace these tools to elevate your sales game and stay ahead in a competitive market.

## SOUND BYTE SUMMARY

— Building your system's structure is a balancing act. Too much rigidity and it won't allow for adaptability to unique buyer needs. Too little could mean a chance to deliver value slips through the cracks and leads to relationship tension.

— Key account planning applies the Pareto Principle to align sales activities with priority relationships.

— Evaluate your pipeline in the context of the sales planning calculator.

— The Seven Pillars of a Great Cadence help to lay the foundation of your communication with prospects.

To get access to all of the templates, frameworks, tools, and podcast episodes referenced in this book, visit this link: **growthforum.io/bonuses**

## NEXT UP

Your efforts to connect with prospects and get potential deals on the right track stand a better chance if you focus on earning the right with value-led communication.

# EARNING THE RIGHT

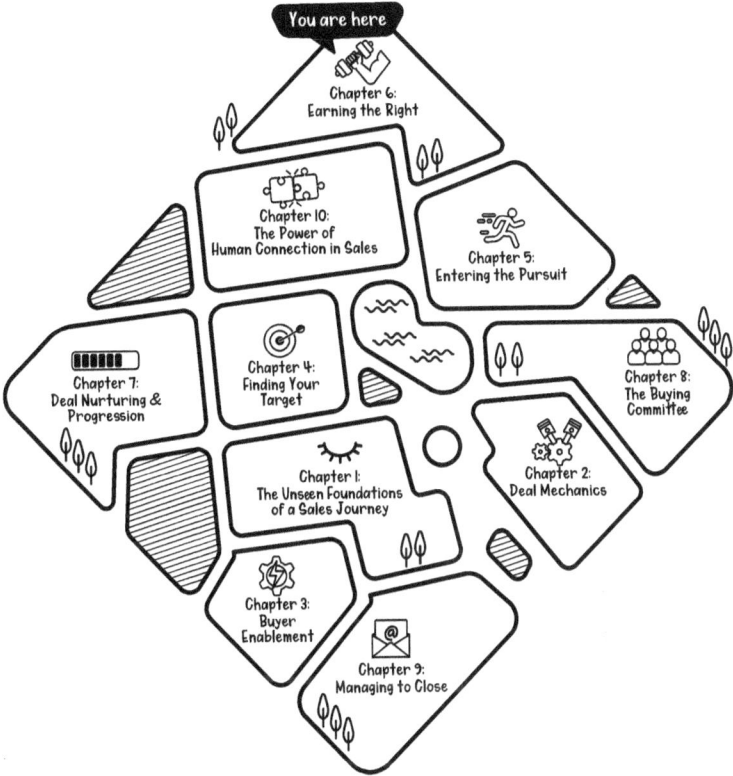

You are here

Chapter 6:
Earning the Right

Chapter 10:
The Power of
Human Connection in Sales

Chapter 5:
Entering the Pursuit

Chapter 7:
Deal Nurturing &
Progression

Chapter 4:
Finding Your
Target

Chapter 8:
The Buying
Committee

Chapter 1:
The Unseen Foundations
of a Sales Journey

Chapter 2:
Deal Mechanics

Chapter 3:
Buyer
Enablement

Chapter 9:
Managing to Close

# What allows you to *earn the right* to talk to prospects?

The thing that people don't want to do but will result in the biggest return is…earning the right.

Regardless of the lead channel, inbound or outbound, and no matter what mediums you use to make first contact, before you can progress any opportunity or go deep into the sales process, *you need to first earn the right.*

Earning the right in the sales process is crucial to building trust and credibility with your prospects. To "earn the right" to engage in deeper sales conversations, a sales professional must start with the way in which a sales professional engages their audience. How they show up with positive intent. With a mindset of helping. With the aim to deliver real insight and value.

Great salespeople earn the right. It's why venture capitalists who used to give startups money for paid advertising now give them money to get a sales rep. They are the new engineers, in terms of value. It's because in some ways sales is more difficult than engineering because it deals with both people and processes.

With that said, this chapter will start with a discussion about understanding motivation before unpacking cold-calling and email strategies to ensure that the buyers you've targeted with your ICP become interested in learning more from you.

## UNDERSTANDING MOTIVATION FIRST

Whether an inbound or outbound lead, we want to understand motivations.

There's a preparation that goes into understanding motivations.

If we don't take the time to think about the types of questions we want to ask, then we're not creating luck for ourselves.

My three magic questions for an inbound lead are:

- What's motivated you to inquire?
- How long have you been considering?
- What's prompted you to take action today?

Now, once we are in a meeting, there are some great questions that sellers can ask. And it's crucial to listen to the buyer's responses. (Check out the Bonus Chapter to see a good example of why.)

Paul Cherry, in *Questions That Sell*, breaks down questions into past, present, and future. Let's take a look, starting with the past-based questions, which according to Cherry typically only make up 10% of questions—there might be an opportunity for sellers to sprinkle just a bit more here during discovery. To access a list of questions we've created, simply go to **growthforum.io/bonuses**.

## Past State

These questions are focused on experiences the buyer has learned from that also draw out situations related to previous problems, current opportunities, and the way their organization purchases.

Examples of past-based questions:

- Walk me through how you handled a similar challenge, and how did you and your team go about managing that challenge?
- How did you go about selecting a provider to help you? (That gives you an indication of their buying process.)
- If you could go back and do that project again, what would you do differently? (That could give you an indication of some of the problems that they encountered and whether their thought process has evolved.)

Past-based questions could maybe help you determine that a buyer might be conditioned a certain way, giving you clues about how they make decisions now. A question about obtaining an allocated budget is a commercial-based question. What other categories of questions can you think of? (Write them down.)

## Current State

This is where the buyer is today. What's going well, the challenges they face, and what's rising to the top in all the problems a business has. With everything they *could* be doing, what are they focusing on? Part of their current state very likely motivated them to book a meeting with you.

Take this scenario, where a Chief Marketing Officer (CMO) and a salesperson go back and forth a bit.

**CMO:** Our sales targets are consistently missed, and we're not sure why.

**Salesperson then asks one of the following:**

- What specific areas of sales are underperforming? (e.g., specific products, regions, channels?)
- What symptoms are you noticing that indicate underperformance (e.g., lower conversion rates, fewer leads, poor marketing response)?
- When did the sales decline start, and what was happening at that time?

**CMO:** Yes, we've particularly been struggling with our latest product line, which hasn't been performing well in the Northeast region.

**Salesperson:** That's helpful to know. When it comes to these underperforming areas, what symptoms have you noticed? Are there issues with conversion rates, or is it more about the volume of leads or perhaps the marketing response?

**CMO:** It seems to be a mix of both, but primarily our conversion rates have dropped significantly. We're getting leads, but they're just not converting at the rate we expected.

**Salesperson:** That sheds more light on the situation. To better understand the timeline, can you recall when this decline began? Was there anything specific happening around that time, such as a change in marketing strategy or a new competitor entering the market?

**CMO:** The decline started about six months ago. We had just launched a major marketing campaign which didn't perform as expected, and around the same time, a new competitor did enter the market with a very aggressive pricing strategy.

**Salesperson:** It sounds like the competitive landscape and the marketing response to your campaign are key factors here. Knowing this, we can explore tailored solutions that address these specific challenges to help improve your conversion rates and overall sales performance.

As you can see from this example, the goal of gathering relevant facts to then better frame the problem and its scope may later set the stage for proposing solutions.

Although we can't spend all our time in the current state, problem validation is one key area to pin down. Why? Because it helps us to develop the business case later on.

You could learn about the impact an indicated problem is having. Maybe there is churn, but there's something *else* happening that is impacting churn. Questions allow you to get the buyer into a zone of thinking and into a higher level perspective, a bird's-eye view of their business.

Our friend Marc talks about lifting oneself up to a 40,000-foot view to see differently. The power of questions allows the buyer to move outside of their normal zone—you are facilitating that adjustment.

The caveat to this is to recognize that the Head of Marketing, who might report into the CMO, is focused on different layers of the business to the CMO. The Head of Marketing may not have a view of strategy, budget allocation, etc., (or they might), whereas the CMO would. On the flip side, asking about EDM might be too in the weeds for a CMO.

Of course, being aware of the org structure *and* the company size is critical to asking a relevant question. If we're talking to an SMB, the strategic question or the detailed question might be appropriate because the marketing org could only be one or two people.

## Future State

The current state is important, but they're not buying today. Yes, they need to tell you there is a problem they're looking to potentially rectify. Is the problem big enough to rectify as well?

But they're buying tomorrow—the future state is why they take action.

Because in that future state, there has to be enough value and enough opportunity that triggers them to say, "You know what? I do want take this leap...I want to choose this path over all the others."

Examples of future state questions:

- What gives this problem priority over the others we've discussed?
- Is your organization ready to go through the pain of change to get there?
- What value does solving this problem unlock?

## THE MAGIC NUMBER

In your preparation, you might look at a set of questions and wonder, *How many should I have ready to ask?*

It's a common question, maybe the most common from sellers and people we coach when it comes to the topic of questioning.

You probably already know the answer: the reality is there is no magic number. You shouldn't really have 10 to 20 questions to ask someone because that will sound like an interrogation. They may be thinking, *Oh my god, I'm just responding and responding and responding.*

This is where the consultative methodology kicks in. Instead of pumping them with questions, start by asking one question. Then, acknowledge their response. If face to face or on a video call, visually nod your head. Say, "Thank you for sharing," confirming what you're hearing and potentially drilling down further.

If you have, say, four or five questions and then you have some drill-downs, you'd be surprised how much information that you can actually capture.

*And then confirming becomes your secret weapon.*

Because by confirming and repeating what you hear, and then drilling down further, all of a sudden you really get an expanded response.

## When to Start Solutioning?

So before even thinking about presenting or starting to push your own agenda, try to drill down a bit. Try to say, "Look, thanks for sharing. I appreciate you opening up about XYZ. Do you mind me asking? Go deeper. Right? Describe the impact it's having across other areas of the business."

If you could actually fix that problem, like, what would it mean for your customers? What would it mean for retention? What would it mean for market share?"

Start to go a bit deeper because, potentially, they might only be looking at that problem on the surface as well. And when you start going a bit deeper, they might start to see that, actually, this problem is having a greater impact than what they initially thought.

### The Unrecognized Need

There's different types of needs that we determine during a sales conversation. There's an obvious need. If it's churn, there still might be an emerging issue that is impacting churn. That's the unrecognized need.

Helping buyers locate that need is great because not only did you help them see the reality of their business situation, but it means you haven't jumped into solutioning before identifying root causes.

## TYPES OF QUESTIONS

A variety of question types and styles bring variety to your questioning and give you flexibility in adapting to certain kinds of buyers.

Question types include permission-based questions and check-based questions.

**Permission-based questions** leverage consultative selling and lower the relationship tension with only a few words and the right tone.

It can simply mean acknowledging information that the buyer shares. For example, on a call, you might say something like, "Hey, thanks for that information."

It can proceed into asking whether you can ask a question to begin with, like this: "The reason for my call is we've got you on the waitlist and we're really excited about that. **Do you mind me asking…**" *then ask the question.*

This kind of lead-in—"Do you mind me asking?"—allows the buyer to say, "No, I don't mind," and then give you the answer. Or they can also say they'd rather not answer. This avoids the buyer not appreciating you asking a certain question. And it's a bit softer than jumping straight to the question. Remember the 55/38/7 split of communication where most of your communication is expression and tone.

We also really like **check-based questions**. Here's what they sound like...

"Thanks for clarifying. Based on what you've said, does it make sense to move to the next step?"

This way we can learn how best to facilitate and guide. Failing to ask this question may make it difficult to progress because we haven't given them a way to progress. But asking this question gives the buyer a chance to say, "Yes, I'm ready!"

## COMMUNICATING VALUE TO YOUR CUSTOMERS

Many common sales tactics create friction against the natural buying cycle.

Friction wastes time and creates relationship tension.

Wasted time is obviously to be avoided.

Relationship tension is usually caused by a lack of trust, which slows things down if not addressed. Because without trust, things just can't progress the same way. It's hard to become a trusted advisor without trust.

Earning the right is about adding and creating value. It's about preparation before every engagement to ensure value is provided. Doing so builds trust. Trust that the seller is there to help the buyer.

As a salesperson, it's about understanding your customers and buyers, what their day to day looks like, what they are trying to do, and what struggles they are having. When you can show that you know how their problem creates a collection of issues across their organization, for just one example, now you've started to speak in a way that shows you care about their time and money.

**Value-based marketing** is a strategic approach that emphasizes the unique benefits and value your product or service offers customers. Instead of focusing solely on your product's features, it centers on understanding and addressing what your ideal customers truly value.

While this effective marketing approach seems simple at first glance, many entrepreneurs often get it wrong. Because of their incorrect perception of value-based marketing, they do more harm than good to their businesses.

By shifting your marketing strategy to highlight these values, however, you can create a stronger connection with your audience and ultimately drive more sales.

## Most Entrepreneurs Get "Value" Wrong

Many entrepreneurs and business owners assume they know what their customers value without actually taking the time to understand their perspectives. An assumption without solid data is a dangerous guessing game. This is why Discovery is not simply a step in the sales process but an ongoing learning process.

Most business owners equate value to tangible features and benefits of their products or services. However, value is subjective and varies widely from one customer to another. What seems valuable to one potential client might differ from another, and value itself can sometimes be affected by intangibles.

If businesses fail to grasp this idea, they can miss the mark in their marketing efforts, leading to missed opportunities and decreased customer satisfaction.

## Knowing What Value Means to Your Customers

To effectively communicate value, you must first understand what value means to your customers. Understanding what is valuable for your ideal customer requires a deep dive into their daily lives, preferences, and pain points.

### Know Their Day-To-Day

Understanding your customers' daily routines and challenges is crucial. This insight allows you to tailor your marketing messages to resonate with their specific needs.

For example, if you're marketing a time-saving kitchen appliance, knowing that your target audience is busy professionals or parents can help you highlight how your product simplifies their daily tasks, likely saving them time.

Understanding a general overview of their daily lives will also allow you to spot trends and patterns in their behavior, giving you valuable insights on positioning your product to align with their value system.

### Interview Real People

What better data to use than real-life customer insights? Conducting surveys and interviews with your existing customers is an excellent way to better understand what they value in your product or service.

You can also ask past or potential customers about their needs, pain points, and what they look for in a product or service like yours.

These conversations will provide valuable information that you can use to refine your marketing messages.

Try sending out an email outreach or direct them to a customer survey after they make a transaction. This way, you can gauge their satisfaction level and gain valuable insights for your marketing efforts.

Continually update your ICPs and Buyer Personas based on these interviews.

### Use AI

Add a prompt into your preferred AI tool, such as ChatGPT, to understand an audience and help to shape your understanding of the persona and ICP.

## How Can You Communicate These Values?

Once you clearly understand what your customers and prospects value, the next step is to communicate these values effectively through your marketing efforts. This part is the hardest, especially if you're used to traditional marketing methods focusing on product features and benefits.

### Customer-Centric Communication

Flip the conversation. Instead of highlighting your product's features, first address your customers' needs and desires. Not asking about what challenges they are facing, or what has changed recently for them, lacks empathy and willingness to discover what they are truly dealing with right now.

Show them you understand their challenges.

**This isn't about providing a solution.**

It's about sharing education and insight that helps them view how they can tackle their problems. Doing this helps them see you as a professional who can guide and educate.

## Listen to Understand

While this tip might seem obvious, truly listening to your customers is crucial. During a cold outreach, many salespeople or business owners worry about how they can insert their sales pitch into the conversation. Look again at the cold-calling script earlier in this chapter for a template you can use and build upon.

Your customers will always know or sense your intentions, and jumping to your sales pitch will only push them away. Instead, listen to what they say, ask open-ended questions, and genuinely try to understand their needs before bringing your offering into the conversation where it makes sense to.

## Focus Less on the Features

As reiterated earlier, value is not solely about the features of your product or service. While it's essential to highlight these features, they should not be the main focus of your marketing efforts.

Instead, emphasize how these features translate into real benefits for your customers' lives. Show them how your product solves their problems or makes their lives easier and more enjoyable, now and in the future.

For a simple B2C example, rather than boring your customer with the technical specifications of your new smartphone, highlight how its long battery life allows them to stay connected and productive on the go.

## Leverage Social Proof

In marketing and sales, there's no stronger proof than social proof. Highlight customer testimonials, quote reviews, and share success stories to showcase the value of your product or service.

Potential customers are more likely to trust and relate to the experiences of their peers rather than a company's claims. Therefore, highlighting positive feedback from satisfied customers can be a powerful tool in communicating value.

## Offer Demonstrations

People are more likely to be convinced when they experience something themselves. Offer product demonstrations or free trials to allow your potential customers to experience the value of your product firsthand.

Let them visualize, or even directly experience, how your product can improve their daily lives and address their specific needs. This way, they can see for themselves how your product can make a significant impact on their lives. This hands-on approach can be more effective than simply telling them about your product's benefits.

Such demonstrations can be particularly effective for salespeople who enjoy live engagement with their customers and prospects.

Remember to do your research! B2B sales is NOT one size fits all. Just because you are the one offering a "free" demo does not mean you have the liberty to waste the buyer's time (which isn't free), and you *should* have researched them as well as be ready to ask specific questions about what they are looking for in their business and in your product—understand the objectives they want to achieve so that the demo, when it's time for that, can be precisely tailored.

## Utilize Case Studies

Case studies provide detailed accounts of how your product or service has successfully addressed specific customer problems—they offer concrete examples of the value you deliver and can be used to illustrate your expertise and effectiveness.

If you're not already doing this, look for a past customer who experienced significant results using your product or service and create a case study around their experience.

This way, you can showcase how your business has helped solve real problems for real people.

Remember Gartner's portrayal of the complex buying journey. These case studies can fit into a buyer experience even before they've met you. Of course, they might also influence the development of a business case, if a buyer is looking for similar results to previous clients.

## Value-Based Marketing Takes Practice

Value-based marketing is not a one-time effort; it requires ongoing practice and refinement. If you're used to sales-centric or product-based marketing, shifting to a value-focused and customer-centric approach may take some time. To help you get started, here are some key practices to keep in mind:

- Continuously gather customer insights through surveys, interviews, and feedback.
- Keep your customers at the center of every marketing or sales decision.
- Regularly update and review your client personas to ensure they align with current market trends and customer needs.

- Incorporate value-focused messaging in all marketing materials, including website copy, social media posts, and email campaigns.
- Leverage social proof through testimonials, reviews, and success stories to showcase the value of your product or service.
- Take some time to personalize your messaging, especially if you're talking to an individual or smaller group.
- Always strive to understand your customer's problems and how your product or service can solve them.

This approach will make it easier to communicate value and build stronger connections with your target audience.

Remember, delivering value is not just about increasing sales; it's about building long-lasting relationships with your customers and making a positive impact on their lives. Keep listening to their needs and adapting your messaging accordingly, and you'll see the results in successful marketing efforts that resonate and progress deals.

## The Value of a Person's Time

Time is precious. Buyers have a limited amount of time. And their time is valuable. We need to earn the right to grab time in their diary.

There will be something in your initial impression or in your cadence that starts to make them feel like you could fill in the trust gap.

Many businesses offer savings of time and money. People are willing to pay for taking things off their plate or to give them efficiencies.

When prospecting and setting up meetings for B2B, the time and money factors are already at play.

Consider a C-suite executive's value on time from a per-hour perspective. How much is 30 minutes of their time? If there are two people you're hoping to speak with, how much is that worth?

Therefore, when reaching out, when making the pitch for such a meeting, these buyers need to have a sense of the value they might get from such a meeting.

Bring a perspective that will make your buyer think differently.

## Why People Won't Meet with You, And Why They Will

If the perceived value is features, product, or their attributes, that's not enough value to justify having time with the prospective buyer because they can get this info on the internet.

However, if you have a position, if you have a point of view, if you have a message as relates to value, then maybe the prospect will take the meeting.

*Stop selling and start educating.*

Use content marketing to create value. Start conversations. Drop a voice chat with a prospect. Message someone in your relationship funnel with a useful article. Understand how to educate in the sales funnel versus the relationship funnel. This boils down to the level of awareness the buyer has and whether they are ready to be in the sales funnel now or if that may come later.

A sales professional mindset needs to focus on the long term. Creating awareness and bridging the trust gap.

| SALES FUNNEL | Relationship type | RELATIONSHIP FUNNEL |
|---|---|---|
| Short term ⌛ | Relationship type | Long term |
| Generating sales | Focuses on | Building relationships |
| Fast | Time to profit | Nurturing relationships |
| Content & pressure tactics to generate sales | Strategies | Relational experience |
| Sales/ROI | Measurable metrics | Relational performance |

To truly educate, understand the buyer and then flip conversation to be value-focused. The engaging message snaps into focus for them. It takes a position for a problem the buyer is tackling.

Flip the script. Think beyond what you do. And focus your attention on what matters to the buyer.

By doing this enough, or with sufficient intensity, you may become a trusted advisor by having an opinion and giving value. (That's what Lui did at News Corp.) Becoming a trusted advisor starts with the mindset of a sales professional. It is moving our motives aside.

Post discovery, every meeting should have an action plan to ensure value is being given and progression in the deal can occur. (Check out the free resources you can access at growthforum.io/bonuses.)

Once in conversations, ask questions, educate buyers, listen actively, tailor the conversation to their needs, and create an experience. (A recent Forrester study said 55% of buyers are influenced by the experience they have with a salesperson, 18% by the brand, 18% the company and product, 9% the price-to-value ratio.)

# CALLING

With all the noise, buyers are ignoring sellers' tactics via email and LinkedIn. That's the easy part of selling: loading up a sequencing tool, adding data from data providers, and then turning on a sequence. So, if buyers are now ignoring their email more than ever before, what should sellers do? This is where the phone kicks in...

Let's start with cold calling.

It's one of the most underused and (for some) scary strategies for generating leads and booking meetings.

For some, there's a reluctance to pick up the phone and dial. Maybe they are more comfortable using email. Maybe there's a fear of making a mistake. Or they simply don't want to. Each of these prevents salespeople from taking action.

If that's you, remember you *can change* and be someone who schedules time, makes the calls, and eventually enjoys and gets a lot of value from calling. Small habits stack up and become second nature. Lean into rejection and learn from it.

We'll now share our tried-and-true strategies, techniques, and tips for successful cold calling, which consistently generates over 20 booked meetings per week with us at Growth Forum.

## Understanding the Basics of Cold Calling

One key aspect to remember when cold calling is the importance of proper preparation. Before picking up the phone, it's critical to research your prospects.

Now, you do not have to spend hours doing research before every call. Instead, know enough about the challenges and opportunities this ICP faces and then go one level deeper. This takes roughly 10–15 minutes on an industry segment within your ICP.

Going one level deeper includes understanding their industry, company background, and any recent news or developments that may impact their business. If they are within your ICP and Buyer Personas, simply review those to save time and to build the habit of keeping them up to date.

By doing so, you can tailor your pitch to resonate with their specific needs and challenges, increasing the likelihood of a successful conversation.

Additionally, effective cold calling requires a confident and engaging communication style.

Your tone of voice, choice of words, and overall demeanor can greatly influence the outcome of the call. Professor Albert Mehrabian found that 7% of communication is what you say, 38% is the tone used, and 55% is nonverbal, mainly one's facial expressions.

It's crucial to say the right things; sound enthusiastic, knowledgeable, and respectful throughout the conversation; and show that through one's body language.

Remember, you only have a short window to capture the prospect's interest, so make every word count.

## Building a Successful Cold-Calling Strategy

According to Seller Signals, buyers who receive a cold call are 82% more likely to consent to a meeting. This is too big an opportunity to miss out on. But to have success with cold calling, you need to have a strong strategy in place, which includes preparation first and foremost. According to LinkedIn, over 80% of B2B decision-makers feel like cold callers are ill-prepared.

Just like mindset is number one (and therefore was Chapter 1), preparation is key for cold calling to work at all. A bad cold call isn't just a no, it's likely to hurt your reputation. A good call, even without an immediate positive response, has the chance to generate returns later on.

Earn the right by being prepared.

Now let's discuss identifying the target audience and building the framework.

## Identifying Your Target Audience

Before you begin making calls, it's important to identify and understand your target audience.

Who are the people that are most likely to be interested in what you offer?

By creating your ICP and Buyer Personas and conducting thorough market research, you can tailor your cold-calling efforts to reach those most likely to convert. You might waste a lot of time if not dialed into a specific list.

Understanding the demographics, psychographics, and behaviors of your target audience is essential. By delving deep into their preferences, pain points, and needs, you can customize your cold-calling approach to resonate with them on a personal level.

This level of understanding allows you to craft a more compelling pitch that speaks directly to their specific challenges and desires.

## Crafting Your Cold-Calling Framework

A well-crafted cold-calling framework is crucial for making a positive impression and engaging your prospects. Your script should be concise, persuasive, and personalized to each individual you are calling.

It should outline the value your product or service offers and address potential pain points or objections. Remember, the goal is to start a meaningful conversation, not to deliver a robotic sales pitch, so use your script more as a guide to help you if you feel like your calls are getting derailed.

What stories are you using to invite your audience into the

conversation? Sharing a relevant anecdote or success story can humanize your pitch and make it more relatable.

By weaving in narratives that illustrate how your offering has positively impacted others, an emotional connection is created. If it resonates really well with prospects, then it can set you apart from the typical sales call.

And yet, some salespeople are resistant to scripts.

"I don't use scripts."

"Scripts don't sound genuine."

If you're in the camp that dislikes using a sales script, try this little exercise.

Record your next 10 calls. Transcribe them. Look for patterns in your language.

It's highly likely you're already following a script without realizing it.

That's why we're big fans of frameworks. A framework allows you to test and review your approach before you even make a call.

Cold calling and prospecting are often viewed as the toughest parts of selling.

What's the main barrier to sellers picking up the phone? Confidence. And confidence comes from competence.

The best way to build competence?

Practice before you dial.

For this, try using apps like Hyperbound.

More importantly, use a framework to guide you through the process. Test it out and fine-tune it. What might need to be added? How will you handle objections and stalls?

If you don't test it before the call, you'll essentially be testing it live.

Here's one to get you started.

## A Simple Cold-Calling Framework

| Connect | | | Pro Tip |
|---|---|---|---|
| Introduce Yourself | Show Them You Know Them | | Mirror voice as best as possible. Pitch and tone are essential in building immediate rapport and understanding the way in which the lead response will help you determine if now is a good time to walk. Always move to the reason or purpose within the first 7 to 12 seconds. Prospect needs to know where you are calling from, what's in it for them and what the ask is. |
| Hi, this is (name) from, the reason for my call is | Referral | (name) suggested we connect | |
| | Trigger | Understand you recently changed roles | |
| | Attribute | Read a LinkedIn post about | |
| Point of View | | | Question |
| Option A: Problem-led point of view. | We are hearing from a lot of (title you are calling) that they are experiencing (pain/problem) which is impacting results. We recently helped (company) achieve (result) | | Do you mind me asking: how is this current trend impacting you? |
| Option B: Outcome-led point of view. | I have some insight into how you can achieve xx results, in a way that fixes xx problem. we have achieved impressive results working with (company) | | Do you mind me asking: how are you currently performing in this area? |
| Go Deeper (if they ask what this is about) | | | Call to Action |
| It's about (what they will achieve) | | | Thanks for sharing. Would it make sense for us to schedule some time so I can share what we have learned and how this could be applied to your business? |

### Connect

Introduce Yourself: Show Them You Know Them

"Hi, this is *NAME* from *COMPANY*, the reason for my call is:

1. Referral: *NAME* suggested we connect
2. Trigger: Understand you recently changed roles
3. Attribute: Read a LinkedIn post about

### Pro Tip:

Mirror voice as much as possible. Pitch and tone are essential in building immediate rapport and understanding the way in which the lead response will help you determine if now is a good time to talk. Always move to the reason or purpose within the first 7–12 seconds. The prospect needs to know where you are calling from, what's in it for them, and what the ask is.

### Point of View

Option A—Problem-Led Point of View: We are hearing from a lot of *TITLE YOU ARE CALLING* that they are experiencing *PAIN/ PROBLEM*, which is impacting results. We recently helped *COMPANY* achieve *RESULT*.

Option B—Outcome-Led Point of View: I have some insight into how you can achieve xx results, in a way that fixes xx problem. We have achieved impressive results working with *COMPANY*.

### Question

Option A—Do you mind me asking, how is this current trend impacting you?

Option B—Do you mind me asking, how are you currently performing in this area?

*Note the permission-based question starting with "Do you mind me asking,…"*

*A similar phrasing would be "May I ask,…"*

### Go Deeper (if they ask what this is about)

It's about WHAT THEY WILL ACHIEVE

### Call to Action

Thanks for sharing, would it make sense for us to schedule some time so I can share what we have learned and how this could be applied to your business?

## Should You Leave a Voicemail?

The answer is a BIG YES.

Why?

Because 80% of first calls will hit voicemail.

Most people won't pick up unknown numbers. Thanks to the flood of scam calls, buyers are already on guard.

But voicemail? It gives you a chance to break through. It lets you leave a real impression. Many buyers have voicemail transcription services, so they will see your voicemail transcribed in text even if they don't listen to the actual voicemail.

With voicemail, you become more than just a number on their screen. You're a person.

So what do you say?

Should you pitch them? Nope.

Leslie Venetz teaches to use the voicemail to guide them and give them a path to respond. Drop your email or mention you're connecting on LinkedIn.

### The Goal Isn't to Get a Callback

And remember, the goal of the voicemail isn't to get a callback. It's to set up the next step in your cadence.

The real hero? The follow-up email. Let them know it's coming. Mention your subject line.

It boosts the chances they'll see it and open it.

## Implementing the Cold-Calling Process

Now that you have a solid strategy in place, it's time to put it into action. Here are two key steps in the cold-calling process:

### Making the First Contact

When making the initial cold call, it's important to be confident, courteous, and respectful of the prospect's time. Introduce yourself, explain the purpose of your call, and ask if it is a good time to talk.

Remember to smile while speaking, as the smile will be "heard" through your tone.

Using a script as a guide rather than a strict set of lines can help you maintain a natural flow of conversation. This approach allows for flexibility in adapting to the prospect's responses and steering the dialogue toward addressing their specific needs.

By being adaptable and responsive, you can better engage the prospect and increase the likelihood of a successful outcome.

### Handling Objections and Rejections

Objections and rejections are common during cold calling. Instead of being discouraged by them, view them as opportunities to address concerns and provide additional information.

Listen carefully to the prospect's objections, empathize with their concerns, and offer solutions or alternative options. By acknowledging their objections as valid points and responding with empathy, you can build trust and credibility.

Moreover, incorporating success stories or case studies into your responses can help illustrate how your product or service has addressed similar concerns for other clients.

This social proof can reassure the prospect of your capability to deliver results, which can alleviate their hesitations.

Additionally, offering a follow-up action, such as sending more information or scheduling a follow-up call, can demonstrate your commitment to addressing their needs and maintaining open communication.

## Enhancing Your Cold-Calling Techniques

In today's digital age, technology can greatly enhance your cold-calling efforts. Here are two ways you can leverage technology to boost your success:

## Using Technology to Boost Cold Calling

There are numerous tools and software available that can streamline and automate various aspects of your cold-calling process.

From CRM systems that help you track leads and manage customer relationships to dialing software that can improve your efficiency, leveraging technology can save you time and improve your overall effectiveness.

Furthermore, incorporating AI into your cold-calling strategy can provide valuable insights and predictive analytics.

AI can analyze data to identify patterns, prioritize leads, and even suggest the best times to call prospects. By leveraging the power of AI, you can make more informed decisions and increase your chances of success in cold calling.

## Essential Skills for Effective Cold Calling

In addition to using technology, developing essential skills is also crucial for effective cold calling. These skills include active listening, effective communication, empathy, and resilience.

By honing these skills and continuously learning and improving, you can become a more confident and successful cold caller.

Mastering the art of objection handling is essential in cold calling.

Anticipating common objections and preparing appropriate responses can help you navigate conversations more smoothly and increase your chances of converting leads into sales.

By practicing objection-handling techniques and adapting them to different scenarios, you can build rapport with prospects and overcome challenges effectively. (More about this in Chapter 9: Managing to Close.)

In reality, many people enjoy working with people who can offer a point of view that answers tough questions. This is the main point of the Challenger Sale, as detailed in the book of the same name.

## Measuring the Success of Your Cold-Calling Efforts

Two ways you can measure your results are through Key Performance Indicators (KPIs) and through feedback:

### Key Performance Indicators for Cold Calling

Tracking KPIs is essential for properly evaluating the effectiveness of your cold-calling efforts.

KPIs, such as the number of calls made, conversion rates, and booked meetings, can provide valuable insights into the performance of your cold-calling campaigns. Use these metrics to identify areas for improvement and make data-driven decisions.

### Improving Your Cold-Calling Strategy Based on Feedback

Lastly, actively seek feedback from your team and prospects to improve your cold-calling strategy. Encourage open communication and regularly review recorded calls or listen to calls in real-time to identify any areas for improvement.

By continuously refining your approach based on feedback, you can optimize your cold-calling efforts and generate even better results.

When measuring the success of your cold-calling efforts, it's crucial to delve deeper into the data.

Beyond tracking the number of calls made and conversion rates, consider analyzing the quality of leads generated through cold calling.

Look at the industries or demographics most responsive to your calls, and tailor your approach accordingly to maximize results.

Also, don't underestimate the power of A/B testing in refining your cold-calling strategy. Experiment with different scripts, call timings, and approaches to see what resonates best with your target audience.

By testing and analyzing the results, you can fine-tune your cold-calling tactics for optimal performance.

Now, having set the table with a phone-led strategy, let's move to email. But first...

---

### Checkpoint 6:
### The Lifelong Skill of Talking on the Phone

*Just as there are checkpoints in a sales and buying journey, there will be checkpoints through this book to test your learning and application: learning without application is simply entertainment.*

### The Sound of Your Voice and How You Made Someone Feel
*Maya Angelou has said: "I've learned that people will forget what you said, people will forget what you did,* **but people will never forget** *how you made them* **feel.***" (emphasis added)*

*Yes, be valuable. Yes, listen. Yes, ask the right question at the right time. But foremost, smile (on the phone) and have good intent. Your smile and intent shine through and change how the buyer experiences the conversation. Make it a bright point in their day. Better yet, make them come to treasure their time with you, even if it is just a three-minute call to give them a touch of value or encouragement.*

---

## EMAILING

Email writing is not just about stringing words together.

But rather a skill that requires finesse and understanding of your target audience.

Mastering the art of email writing involves more than just crafting messages; it requires a deep understanding of human psychology and communication dynamics.

Learn the intricacies of how your audience perceives and responds to written communication, then tailor your emails to resonate with them on a deeper level.

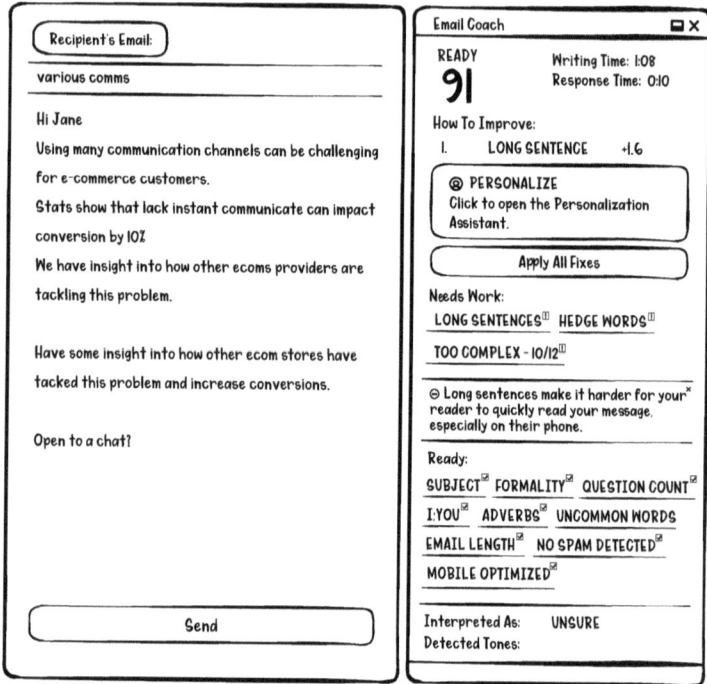

Tool: Lavender AI Email Assistant is one of our favorites in helping us to write quality emails.

## The Importance of a Strong Subject Line

The subject line is the first impression your email makes, so make it count.

If it's too long, a buyer may not be able to see it in their browser or mobile device.

A strong subject line should be concise, compelling, and provide a clear value proposition. Consider using powerful words, personalization, or intriguing questions to grab your reader's attention.

Understanding the science behind attention-grabbing subject lines can significantly improve your email open rates.

By using elements like emotional triggers, curiosity gaps, and social proof, you can increase the chance of your emails being noticed and opened by recipients.

## Crafting a Compelling Email Body

After hooking your reader with an irresistible subject line, it's time to deliver on the promise. To create a compelling email body, keep it short and focus on providing value.

Use bullet points, subheadings, and bold text to break up the content and make it easier to skim. (Again, remember many buyers will be reading at least some of your emails on a mobile device.)

Leveraging storytelling techniques in your email body can evoke emotions and create a more engaging experience for the reader.

## The Power of a Clear Call to Action

To maximize the impact of your B2B sales emails, be sure to include a crystal clear call to action (otherwise known as a CTA).

Whether it's scheduling a demo, downloading a white paper, or signing up for a free trial, make it easy for your prospects to take the next step.

Use action-oriented language and provide a sense of urgency to prompt immediate action.

Additionally, A/B testing different CTAs and analyzing the data can help you optimize your email campaigns for better conversion rates.

By experimenting with various wording, placement, and design elements of your CTAs, you can uncover insights that drive more meaningful engagement with your audience.

As a caveat, it's not always necessary to use a call to action on every email.

## The Psychology Behind Winning Emails

Effective B2B sales emails go beyond persuasive writing.

They tap into the psychology of your prospects and build trust.

Understanding the psychology behind winning emails is crucial for crafting messages that resonate with your audience.

By diving into the intricacies of human behavior and decision-making, you can tailor your email content to trigger the desired responses from your recipients.

A deep understanding of psychological principles can elevate your email marketing strategy to new heights, from leveraging cognitive biases to appealing to emotional triggers.

## Building Trust Through Your Emails

Trust is the foundation of any successful business relationship.

In your emails, demonstrate your expertise, highlight success stories, and provide social proof.

Sharing case studies from satisfied customers to inspire confidence and establish credibility.

Transparency and authenticity play a pivotal role in fostering trust through email communication.

Clearly communicate your intentions, be honest about your offerings, and show genuine interest in solving your prospects' pain points.

By cultivating a trustworthy image through your emails, you can lay a solid groundwork for long-term relationships with your clients.

## The Role of Persuasion in Email Writing

Persuasion can be seen as an art and a science, and using it strategically in your B2B sales emails can significantly improve your conversion rates.

Use the principles of persuasion, such as scarcity, reciprocity, and social proof, to nudge your prospects toward taking action.

But remember, always be authentic and genuine in your approach.

In addition to the traditional principles of persuasion, incorporating elements of storytelling can also enhance the effectiveness of your emails.

By crafting compelling narratives that resonate with your audience's experiences at an emotional level, you can create a powerful connection that drives engagement and boosts conversion rates.

Some might question whether emotional manipulation is needed. But few question when they are provided new information that helps them with something they were struggling with.

So long as the storytelling is honest, it adds a human touch to your emails, making them more relatable and impactful for your recipients.

## The Anatomy of B2B Sales Emails

Understanding the fundamental differences between B2B and B2C emails is crucial for crafting successful campaigns.

When delving into the world of B2B sales emails, it's important to understand the intricate dynamics at play.

Unlike B2C emails that target individual consumers, B2B emails are tailored to appeal to businesses.

This distinction shapes the tone, content, and strategy employed in crafting compelling email campaigns.

Within the realm of B2B sales emails, precision and strategy reign supreme. Decision-makers are the primary audience, individuals who hold the power to influence purchasing decisions within their organizations.

It's super important to address their specific pain points and needs with a laser-focused approach. By customizing your messaging to resonate with these key stakeholders, you establish credibility and trust, paving the way for meaningful business relationships.

## The Difference Between B2B and B2C Emails

In B2B sales, you are typically targeting decision-makers who have specific pain points and needs.

Tailor your messaging accordingly and focus on the business value your product or service brings. Avoid gimmicks or overly informal language that may undermine your professionalism.

Furthermore, the distinction between B2B and B2C emails extends beyond the target audience to encompass the very essence of communication.

B2B emails thrive on a foundation of professionalism and expertise, requiring a nuanced approach that highlights the tangible benefits and solutions offered.

Unlike B2C emails that may leverage emotional triggers or impulse buying, B2B emails rely on a strategic alignment of business objectives and value propositions.

## Key Elements of Successful B2B Sales Emails

Successful B2B sales emails have a few essential elements in common.

Personalization, relevancy, and a clear value proposition are key.

Customize your email templates for each prospect, demonstrate an understanding of their challenges, and clearly articulate how your solution can solve their problems. Knowing how and when to use automation matters. (With great power comes great responsibility.)

With that said, personalization lies at the heart of effective B2B sales emails, serving as a powerful tool to establish rapport and connection with potential clients.

By tailoring your messages to address the specific needs and pain points of each prospect, you demonstrate a genuine interest in their success. More so, a clear and compelling value proposition is essential to cut through the noise of the digital landscape. (Refer to your ICP/Buyer Personas!)

Articulating how your product or service can deliver tangible results and address critical business challenges is key to capturing the attention of busy decision-makers.

## Strategies for Effective Email Follow-Ups

You have to follow up. But how much?

Following up with prospects is an integral part of the sales process. But how can you make your follow-up emails effective and avoid seeming pushy?

Establishing a personalized connection with your prospects can significantly enhance the effectiveness of your follow-up emails.

Reference details from previous interactions or mention common interests to show that you value the relationship beyond just making a sale. This personal touch can help you stand out in a crowded inbox and increase the likelihood of a positive response.

### Timing Your Follow-Up Emails

The timing of your follow-up emails can greatly impact their effectiveness.

Avoid bombarding your prospects with multiple emails in rapid succession.

Instead, space them out strategically, considering factors such as their buying cycle, industry events, or specific triggers that may indicate their readiness to engage.

Furthermore, leveraging automation tools can streamline the process of timing your follow-up emails. Again, do so wisely. Buyers are good at spotting lazy automation, and this doesn't bode well for you.

However, one way to use automation intelligently is to set up automated triggers based on prospect behavior or engagement levels: this way you can ensure that your emails reach them at the most opportune moments, increasing the chances of a meaningful interaction.

### Content for Follow-Up Emails

When crafting follow-up emails, provide additional value or information that your prospects will find useful. We like to organize content themes that align with the buyer journey and their stage of awareness.

Before going deeper into the buyer's journey, it's helpful to share relevant content, such as industry reports, case studies, or success stories.

By offering valuable insights without a hard sales pitch, you can position yourself as a trusted advisor rather than a pushy salesperson.

Also, incorporating interactive elements into your follow-up emails can boost engagement and encourage prospects to take action. Consider including clickable calls-to-action, interactive surveys, or personalized product recommendations to make your emails more dynamic and compelling.

By catering to different learning and engagement styles, you can cater to a wider audience and increase the impact of your follow-up strategy.

### Measuring the Success of Your Email Campaigns

Tracking the effectiveness of your email campaigns is crucial for optimizing your B2B sales strategy and achieving better results.

### Key Metrics to Track

Metrics such as open rates, click-through rates, and conversion rates are indicators of your email's success.

Analyze these metrics to identify areas for improvement and experiment with different approaches.

Keep an eye on your unsubscribe rate as well, as it can provide insights into the relevance and effectiveness of your email content.

### Interpreting Email Analytics

Interpreting email analytics requires a holistic approach.

Look beyond the numbers and identify patterns or trends.

Use A/B testing to compare different subject lines, email formats, or CTAs and learn what resonates best with your target audience.

By understanding the art of email writing, leveraging psychological principles, and mastering the key elements of B2B sales emails, you can create campaigns that win over prospects and drive results.

As you refine your strategy, don't be afraid to experiment, learn from successful examples, and adapt your approach accordingly. Writing can be hard sometimes, so try to have fun with it…Happy emailing!

## SOUND BYTE SUMMARY

___ If you don't understand the buyer's motivation, then it is more difficult to gain their trust—ask past-, current-, and future-state questions to show your curiosity and earn the right.

___ Cold-calling frameworks allow you to reduce stress and build confidence, and success, on the phone.

___ Emails are critical for information flow across time and the deal itself.

To get access to all of the templates, frameworks, tools, and podcast episodes referenced in this book, visit this link: **growthforum.io/bonuses**

## NEXT UP

Nurturing and progression help the buyers move from awareness to consideration and eventually to decision, with the business case driving the discussion and flow of the deal. Buyers who codevelop and cocreate the business case are more likely to want to get the deal to the finish line.

# NURTURING & PROGRESSION

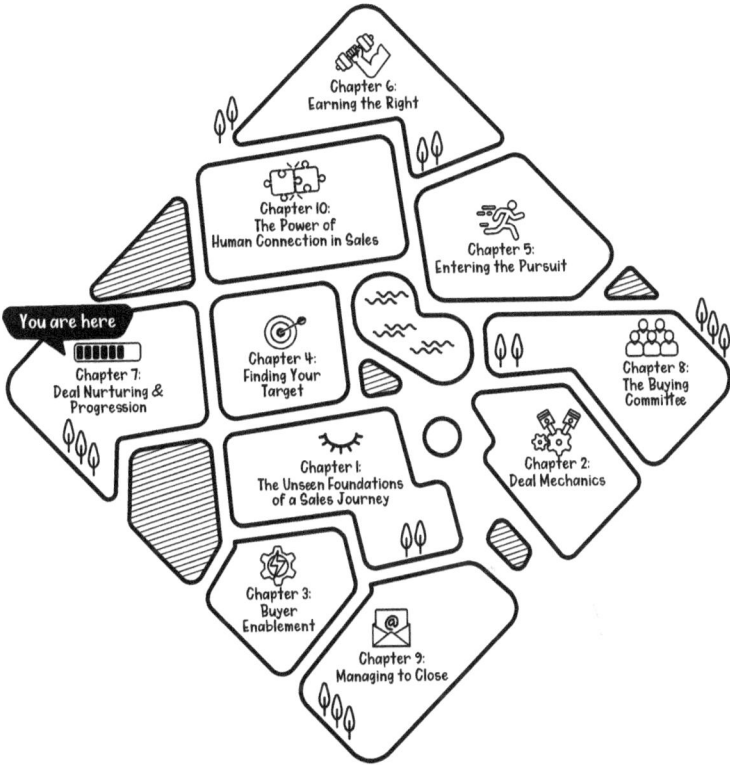

You are here

Chapter 6:
Earning the Right

Chapter 10:
The Power of
Human Connection in Sales

Chapter 5:
Entering the Pursuit

Chapter 7:
Deal Nurturing &
Progression

Chapter 4:
Finding Your
Target

Chapter 8:
The Buying
Committee

Chapter 1:
The Unseen Foundations
of a Sales Journey

Chapter 2:
Deal Mechanics

Chapter 3:
Buyer
Enablement

Chapter 9:
Managing to Close

An exploration of tactics
to *nurture and progress deals* at a
comfortable pace and rhythm.

I f you only focus on leads who are ready to buy…
You'll miss out on a LOT of sales.

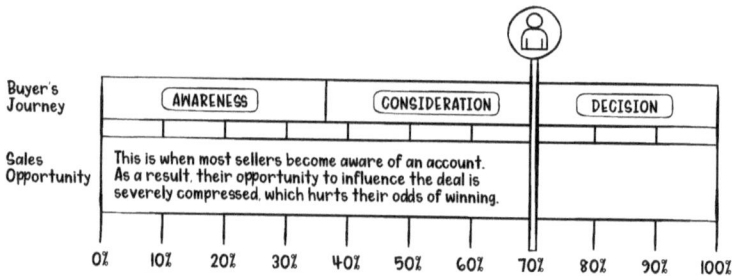

Fact: the majority of leads aren't prepared to make a purchase.

But this does not mean they won't buy. They simply won't buy just yet.

This means you have to approach them differently. And that boils down to one word:

**Nurturing.**

You want to nurture your leads by educating them. Giving and creating so much value for them, so when they are ready to buy…

…guess who pops up in their mind?

Our point exactly.

The overall nurturing process is layered into the offer process, as shown here.

From pre-meeting preparation all the way through to next steps, let's see exactly how to facilitate a deal in the context of nurturing and progression.

The point of preparation is to develop a **point of view** that will be expressed to the buyer and to anticipate objections they will have, given their level of awareness and where they are in the buying journey. The right questions at the right time will allow a conversation to develop, which moves things along in a productive manner, showing that you, as the seller, are always listening and seeking to fill their information gaps, ultimately bringing value every time you engage.

## FIRST MEETING:
## THE WAY YOU PREPARE IS HOW YOU WIN

You've probably heard us say, "The foundation to success is preparation," and that's true for the first meeting as well—it is set up by your preparation.

Use the Discovery: Pre-Call Planner found in the bonuses section to ensure you can:

- Be laser-focused by knowing your prospect in and out before dialing
- Develop a **point of view** or perspective
- Ask the right questions to uncover hidden needs and pain points effortlessly
- Feel confident walking into the call (your state will come through in your tone and nonverbal communication)
- Close more deals by turning conversations into conversions—the first impression during discovery goes a long way to establishing a trusted advisor status

### Key Steps for Effective Meetings

Before the meeting, research the prospect's company, industry, and major challenges. Understand the prospect's persona, focusing on key highlights about their role, and develop a tailored point of view for the discussion.

The buyer profile is basic but important. Are you talking to the Champion, an Anti-Sponsor? A quick check of LinkedIn to see what they've been up to helps.

Then, develop your **point of view**. This will be the overall key perspective to bring. You are helping a number of buyers like them in various areas. Your insight-led prospecting has led you to them.

During the meeting, begin by setting a clear agenda and explaining the purpose. "The purpose of this meeting is XYZ." Lay out the structure, including the timing. Before diving into the core of the meeting, also ask, "Is there anything else you'd like me to cover?"

Offer immediate value by sharing insights or relevant information that will benefit the prospect. Use thoughtful, open-ended questions to uncover their motivations and underlying issues. Confirm your understanding by referencing success stories and outlining next steps.

Leverage the Three Ws to guide the conversation: clarify the purpose of the meeting, explain what's in it for the prospect, and set a time frame. Always confirm any additional topics that need to be addressed.

Throughout the meeting, ask insightful questions that encourage meaningful dialogue, steering away from leading questions. Use real-world stories and examples from similar situations to build trust and credibility, providing social proof of successful outcomes. Anticipate potential objections and be ready with strategies to address them.

To conclude, identify the key takeaways—whether it's the problem impact, future outcomes, KPIs, or business implications—and establish clear next steps. Ensure there is a concrete action plan to drive results. It's not always necessary to have the full prospect "state of play" (use case, problem and impact, future state outcome, ROI, and prospect overall KPI), but getting at least two to three of these is recommended.

## Cautionary Considerations

Build rapport and trust before discussing sensitive or commercial details. Avoid rushing the qualification process—take time to earn the right to ask probing questions. Be attentive to the prospect's comfort level and their meeting environment.

## Efficiency Tips

Customize a pre-meeting planner to fit your business model. Understand the prospect's organizational structure and decision-making process beforehand. Start with smaller opportunities to implement a "land and expand" approach for growing the account. Finally, act on the insights gathered from the meeting to drive results and use community support to ensure consistent application of your pre-meeting strategy.

## Post-Discovery Brief

After the call, it's time to keep the conversation flowing logically and to continue to facilitate the buyer through their journey.

Also available in the bonuses, our Post-Discovery Brief focuses on the current state and the desired state. Because it's a live document between the prospect and you, the seller, it allows for the start of collaboration and investment from the buyer to help you understand where they want to go, all in an asynchronous communication layer.

Basic sections to include are the Executive Summary, Problem Statement, Next Steps, Current State, Desired State, and Suggested Roadmap.

By listing out the bullets for the Current State and Desired State, a priority can be developed as well.

With the Desired State in place, a Roadmap can be drafted to achieve that outcome.

### Future Calls

As conversations progress, continue to send post-call briefs that include the Current State, Desired State, and Roadmap. A framework for these ongoing post-call briefs is also available in the bonuses section on Growth Forum (found at the end of this chapter).

We want the prospect to work on this with us. The IKEA Effect (described in the coming pages) proves that investment in the building of something leads those involved to value it higher.

During the Discovery Call, a business case will start to come into view...

## BUSINESS CASE VALIDATION

The idea of developing a business case is central to being customer-focused as a seller.

The business case is one of the most valuable documents to create alongside buyers. It not only sets sellers up as trusted advisors, but it involves the Buying Committee in developing the solution they want to adopt in the language that makes sense for their business.

Great rapport, connection, and trust is of little use without the business case tailored to the specific needs of the buyers. The commercial ROI is necessary to nail down.

With this in mind, the communication surrounding the nurturing and progression of deals will be discovering, learning, developing, and honing the business case—as well as selling it internally (more on this in Chapter 8: The Buying Committee).

A successful cadence nurtures deals while ensuring a high probability of progression and accounting for the particular stage in the buyer's journey and each member of the Buying Committee.

It starts with business case development and validation. That can only happen if we truly know what the buyers and the business need.

What makes a great business case?

What steps are needed to build one?

Recall from the News Corp story that Luigi built the business case slowly with an internal team after doing hands-on research on the factory floor in the overnight hours for two weeks straight, which led to him becoming a trusted advisor.

Generally speaking, business case development begins quite early. This gives it time to evolve as the Buying Committee comes onboard and questions are asked internally.

We like to send the business case post the first meeting.

The business case will need to show you understand the buyer, the customer, the company, their market space, and how the solution drives toward a commercial ROI.

Get them involved in the cocreation process right away, because of the power of...

## The IKEA Effect

Remember the IKEA Effect. Between those who buy furniture prebuilt versus those who assemble it themselves, the latter group valued the furniture higher.

Same goes for working alongside your champion and others within the buying committee to codevelop, cocreate, and collaborate as the business case comes together through the validation stages.

This is so important that we recommend including specific sales steps to bring additional stakeholders into meetings to do just that.

Try saying this at the end of a call with your champion: "Typically at this stage we like to bring in a few others and have a roundtable discussion to see whether there's alignment and whether we can facilitate this for you."

## NURTURE THROUGH EDUCATION

Nurturing leads is an essential aspect of your sales operating system. Many of your leads will enter this stage, and when they do it's crucial to help them progress through a logical and persuasive approach.

The relationship you build with your pipeline is an investment. It's not a one-off investment but a continuous one...

And the returns compound with time.

Cadences that provide value to specific buyers means they not only think of you when it comes time to consider buying, but also that they are as aware as possible of the problem space that your solutions address.

Since most prospects are not ready to buy today, staying top of mind through education-focused content is really the simplest way to stay connected because people enjoy learning something new, especially when relevant to what they do each day.

Providing education can happen manually, too (within a cadence). Why not drop a voice message or a link to a great article? With these, no call to action is necessary. It's mainly keeping the communication open.

This simple tactic works in the relationship funnel as well, which we have touched briefly in Chapter 6: Earning the Right and will again in Chapter 10: The Power of Human Connection.

But when it comes to your sales pipeline, the business case is really what is going to drive momentum.

### Calls to Action Not Always Necessary

Sometimes the best call to action is NO call to action.

We love to drop a note or a voice note with a link to an article that might be helpful to a prospect. This one isn't easy to automate, but it tends to have a high response rate.

It can also be used to pick up on a high-value lead that didn't resonate with the original sequence.

When it comes to the relationship funnel, leaving *out* a call to action works quite well.

If you want to do a very light call to action, use something like: "Hey, when you're ready, you can connect with me *here*."

## MANAGING COMMON DEAL DYNAMICS

It's common to have a situation where the Champion is ready to move fast.

That's great on the one hand, because having at least one enthusiastic and effective Champion is necessary.

On the other hand, if the champion isn't aware of the dynamics of other buyers and stakeholders, it may be necessary for you as the seller to help to facilitate.

Your instincts and experience with basic emotions and fears, as well as with using a variety of communication techniques with the DiSC profile, will aid you.

In the DiSC model, it often occurs that the I is ready to jump out of the plane but the C is not. This will mean managing the I's expectations while the C is further prepped.

If you're a soccer fan, this looks like Chiellini pulling Saka back in the Euro 2020 Final.

When stakeholders are in tension—one ready to go, the other not —it is the unanswered questions that become the deal-killer.

The critical unanswered questions are usually related to the business case.

## Checkpoint 7:
## What Have YOU Taken Ownership For?

*Just as there are checkpoints in a sales and buying journey, there will be checkpoints through this book to test your learning and application: learning without application is simply entertainment.*

### The IKEA Effect in Your Own Sales OS Journey

*The idea of investing in your own learning, of taking responsibility for the way you approach selling, for building your personal sales system, that is the IKEA Effect at work in your own learning. Take a moment to reflect on the changes you've already made to your sales system. Pick something simple: Maybe you added one of the nine stages from Chapter 3: Deal Mechanics that was missing (or in dire need of improvement). Maybe you upped your intent to provide value when on prospecting cold calls. Maybe you've found ways to change your mindset, which has had an umbrella effect on the rest of your process. Make a note of the change and let's get back into it!*

## HOW TO MANAGE AND WIN STALLED DEALS

If a deal is progressing really well and it's ticking, you're qualifying, they've defined a problem, they've said yes, the return on investment there, but then it gets stuck, it's our job to *not* try to force it through, it's our job to seek understanding of what's causing it to get stuck.

Pipeline does not pay the bills. Closed/won deals pay the bills.

When deals start getting stuck and the time to close increases, that starts to indicate a problem.

Most people, when they see stalled deals, try to close the deal—by following up.

That can create tension when the other person, the buyer, isn't ready to receive.

And yet, it is possible to implement effective follow-up strategies for stalled deals in order to revive them and move them forward in the sales process.

## Start with the Buyer

The buyer meets with a salesperson because they have a problem.

The first meeting with the salesperson goes well—the buyer learns something new and develops it further. Maybe they even develop the business case. The problem is even found to affect other parts of the business. Costing the company a lot. They decide to tackle it.

Now, if they become a champion and have to sell upward through a hierarchical structure, it's possible that one level up isn't convinced it is a priority.

Even if the buyer has had a very positive experience with the seller, they might not feel great about coming back to the seller with the bad news: "You know what, even though we had a great conversation, it's not right for the business right now."

That's the most common example of a stalled deal when using the champion entry method.

## As a Seller—Seek Understanding

Not every buyer will buy what you're selling often, so they may need guidance about how to help you sell that internally, especially with the champion or endorsement model of selling.

So the question for you the seller is, what stopped the momentum? It's not that we will ask this directly. But we are trying to learn more about this.

Instead of trying to push the deal and trying to follow up, *seek understanding first*, because something is causing the progress to stop.

From a plumber's perspective, a clogged pipe will be investigated, for instance with a camera. That's seeking understanding, just like sellers should do.

Don't try to force anything through.

## It's the *Way* that You Follow Up

Careful about follow up, follow up, follow up…just for the sake of following up.

You might have to go *back* in the process.

Maybe a new stakeholder has gotten involved who doesn't understand the full business case or why the investment is being made at all.

Of course, follow-up is essential to progress deals. So we are not saying not to follow up.

But it's the *way* in which you do.

If we're working with a champion that didn't have alignment with the next level up decision-maker, we may have to ask thoughtful questions—questions that they actually *can't* answer. This way, they have to do research and seek input.

## Balance the Emotion that Exists

Have you ever avoided a tough conversation?

Sometimes it's easier to avoid it than have the tough but necessary discussion.

That's true for both buyer and seller—both humans.

Now, you, the seller, want to close.

Maybe the pipeline is weak. Or you're an independent contractor and this deal means a lot.

But it's important to isolate that emotion.

Change the way that you're looking at this deal.

Instead of thinking and feeling that *I need this deal*, let's update our perspective.

Remember the nightclub drink navigation scene we spoke about before? Instead of seeing yourself as carrying a tray of drinks from the bar through the crowded dance floor to your friends, change your perspective...

Imagine you are in the balcony, able to see all the gaps—and you can speak in an earpiece to the one carrying all those drinks. *That's* the perspective you need to have when it comes to stalled deals as well.

Before moving on, let's recap what we've learned.

### Key Steps

1. **Identify the Reason for the Project:** Start your follow-up by reminding the client of the key reason or project that they were seeking to solve or achieve. This helps to bring focus back to the initial goal.

2. **Ask Thoughtful Questions:** Instead of generic follow-up emails, ask questions that require the client to provide more in-depth information about their current status or any changes that may have occurred.

3. **Provide Value:** Ensure that every follow-up email provides value to the client. Offer insights, solutions, or recommendations that can help them make progress.

4. **Consider a Takeaway Approach:** If the client is unresponsive, consider using a takeaway approach where you mention reallocating resources due to lack of

response. This can trigger action from the client. (Do this thoughtfully to preserve the relationship.)

5. **Be Prepared to Walk Away:** If necessary, be prepared to walk away from a deal that is not progressing. Protect your time and energy by valuing your own worth.

## Cautionary Notes:

- Avoid using manipulative tactics or creating false scarcity. Be genuine and respectful in your communication.
- Be prepared for the possibility of losing a deal when using a takeaway approach. Not all clients may respond positively to this strategy.

## Tips for Efficiency:

- Prioritize deals that have the potential to close soon and focus your follow-up efforts on those.
- Review your pipeline regularly to identify stalled deals and take action promptly to either revive them or remove them from the pipeline.
- Engage in brainstorming sessions with your team to come up with creative follow-up strategies for different scenarios, especially those that if improved have an outsized impact.

By following these steps and guidelines, you can effectively navigate stalled deals, improve client engagement, and increase the chances of closing deals successfully.

In closing this section, keep in mind that we have touched on emotions and how to balance them. In the next section, we will dive a bit deeper into one of the strongest emotions there is: fear.

## REDUCTION OF FEAR AND ANXIETY
## IN DECISION-MAKING

One key element of selling is influencing people to take action with you.

But even if you have a great business case and your nurturing is effectively progressing deals, that doesn't mean those deals will get to a satisfying conclusion.

Once you've dialed in your lead generation and attention to the buyer's journey, the next step is to do what you can to address objections during the nurturing and progression phases, when buyers are truly considering what you have to offer as a solution to their pain points and preparing to make an investment. (Additional objections will arise during the bottom-of-the-funnel conversations—these will be discussed in Chapter 9.)

At their core, many objections stem from the fear and anxiety that buyers feel about making a purchase decision.

It's the emotional layer of decision-making that often precedes rational thought.

Whether it's the fear of making the wrong choice, losing money, or dealing with the unknown, these psychological hurdles can be major roadblocks.

If you can't find a way to ease those fears and worries, you'll likely lose that potential customer's interest faster than you can say, "But wait, there's more!"

How can we surface the true objection below the surface?

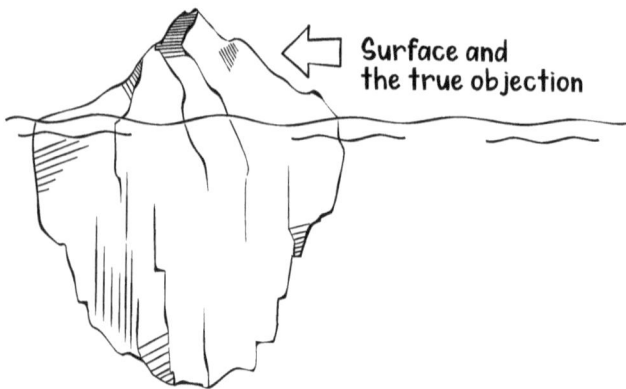

Surface and the true objection

When you can learn to put your prospects' minds at ease—often through mirroring—and by listening *first*, you can instil the confidence buyers need to take action. This way, fewer deals stall out, and better deals get done.

Let's see how to use risk-reversal tactics and to further build credibility and trust.

## The Root Causes of Fear and Anxiety in Purchasing Decisions

You can't overcome something until you understand it first, right?

Let's take a look at some of the major fears and psychological factors that can make your prospects so hesitant to whip out their wallets.

### Common Fears in Purchasing Decisions

One of the biggest fears prospects have is simply making the wrong choice. Whether it's picking the wrong product, service, or vendor, nobody wants to end up with buyer's remorse. That nagging voice in the potential customer's head wonders, "What if there's something better out there?" or "What if I'm missing out on a better deal?"

Then there's the fear of financial loss. Even if prospects can afford your offering on paper, parting with their hard-earned cash isn't easy. Lingering doubts about whether it will be worth the investment can put the brakes on quickly.

Another major roadblock is the fear of change or the unknown. Your prospect may be comfortable with their current situation, tools, or processes. Adopting something new (no matter how promising) brings a level of uncertainty they may want to avoid.

### Psychological Factors Contributing to Decision Paralysis

Now, let's talk about some core psychological principles at play here.

Loss aversion, for example, means we tend to value avoiding losses more than acquiring gains. So the perceived potential loss or risk often outweighs the potential benefits in a buyer's mind.

Confirmation bias can also rear its ugly head, where people favor information that confirms their existing beliefs or assumptions.

Finally, there's choice overload—the more options available, the more overwhelming and paralyzed prospects may feel. If your buyers are doing their research, they may have already felt this and could be leaning on you, the seller, to ease this overwhelm.

We can go on and on, but the bottom line is this:

There are real, deep-seated factors driving these fears in your buyers' minds.

**Luckily, you're about to learn how to neutralize them.**

### Crushing That Fear:
### Risk-Reversal Tactics to Ease Your Prospects' Minds

When fears about making the wrong choice or losing money are looming large, sometimes people need a big confidence boost to hit the "buy" button.

That's where risk-reversal tactics can be total game-changers.

### Money-Back Guarantees

Let's start with the classic money-back guarantee. By removing that financial risk entirely, you're instiling a huge sense of confidence and security in your buyers. The message is clear: "Try our product, and if you don't absolutely love it, you'll get every penny back—no questions asked."

But there's an art to crafting a compelling guarantee. You'll want it to be prominently displayed and emphasize attributes like:

- A generous timeframe (30, 60, 90 days or more)
- Hassle-free returns with no restocking fees
- Your company's commitment to 100% satisfaction— a rock-solid guarantee can swiftly obliterate objections and put minds at ease.

### Free Trials and Samples

*Note that the following approach may have limited scope for complex B2B deals, and yet there may be a way to think differently about your offering...*

Have you ever wondered why every law firm offers a free consultation? There's something to it.

It may not make the firm any money, but a free consultation does get enough feet through the firm's doors to generate clients. With enough consultations, law firms let the law of averages work its magic.

This is what free trials and samples can do for you.

Samples and trials let prospects experience your product firsthand through free trials or samples. This gives them a risk-free, commitment-free way to see what you're all about before pulling out their wallets.

Whether it's a free 14-day software trial, a sample box of products, or a test drive of your service, you're eliminating the unknown and building crucial trust. If customers can kick the tires themselves and see the value, that fear starts melting away.

## Leverage Social Proof

Speaking of trust, don't underestimate the power of testimonials and social proof to settle doubts.

Having others who've used your solution rave about their positive experience—or even simply speak honestly about its limitations and benefits—can be incredibly reassuring to skeptical prospects. (Some buyers see a red flag if something feels too good to be true.)

You might highlight glowing reviews, case studies of major clients, or quotes from loyal customers about how your product transformed their lives or businesses.

When people see others like them finding success, those psychological hurdles start to crumble.

Social proof also can play into the fear of missing out and loss aversion in general, although it is good to balance the presentation of social proof of this kind with the positive feeling that comes with added trust and credibility.

List of awards and company logos ("as seen in") already using the product or service are a nice way to showcase that others already trust and value what you're doing.

## Building Trust and Credibility

At the end of the day, making a purchase often comes down to one key factor: how much your prospect trusts you and your brand.

Without that foundation of credibility, fears and doubts will persist, but there are some surefire ways to boost confidence and nudge your prospects to a purchase.

### Transparency and Honest Communication to Give the Buyer Control

Let's start with the basics: being upfront, transparent, and honest in all your messaging and interactions. This means avoiding any whiff of shady marketing tactics or overhyped claims that could erode trust.

Instead, address common concerns and objections head-on. Don't try to sweep issues under the rug.

Own up to potential downsides or limitations but focus on how your solution overcomes them.

This level of authentic communication goes a long way.

The key layer of this is that it gives the buyer a feeling of control. Since *lack of control* makes buyers feel internal resistance, the consultative selling approach helps them to feel in control the entire time. A very simple way to do this is to provide pricing or subscription options or a mutual action plan to reference between touchpoints.

### Demonstrate Your Expertise

One of the best ways to build credibility is by showcasing your genuine expertise and authority in your industry or niche. If prospects see you as the go-to leader they can trust, that often means leads will be more comfortable progressing.

Start by highlighting key credentials, certifications, awards, or accolades your company or team has earned. You can also create content that positions you as a knowledgeable expert, whether that's:

- An authoritative blog or vlog
- Speaking at conferences or events
- Hosting webinars or virtual summits
- Appearing as a guest expert on podcasts

The more you can establish your competency, the more those fears will fade into the background. Bear in mind that the buyer's ability to verify your claims easily will matter and that those that respect such credentials are translating those credentials into a level of security in choosing you to help them. Word of mouth travels quickly, so it goes without saying: be honest about what you've accomplished—embellishment doesn't pay.

All of the above can also be seen as offering something for free. Doing so is a great way to activate the power of reciprocity. Humans have an inherent desire to reciprocate when they receive something of value. Give, give, give, and this will trigger a psychological need to return the favor.

### Make Security and Reliability a Priority

For many buyers, fears around safety, security, and reliability loom large—especially with bigger, higher-stakes purchases. Prospects need to be utterly confident your product or service is robust, stable, and secure.

So be sure to highlight things like:

- Your commitment to data privacy and protection
- Robust quality-control processes
- Resilient technology infrastructure
- Rigorous security audits and certifications

Spell out the reliable, battle-tested nature of what you offer. The more transparent you can be about prioritizing safety, performance, and competent delivery, the more those anxieties will dissipate.

### Selling the Change—Not the Product

Do you know what's even more powerful than selling a product? Selling the transformation that product can bring. It's not what you're selling but the outcome you're helping the buyer to achieve. Remember, often, that is simply *change*.

When you can vividly paint a picture of how a buyer's life or business will be better after using what you offer, that's when fears take a backseat to excitement.

Often, the vision of the transformation will take hold above and beyond the commercial business case.

### Use Before-and-After Content

One of the best ways to highlight a transformation is through compelling before-and-after content.

Whether it's photos, videos, data points, or customer stories, give prospects a glimpse of the struggle they're in now and what's possible when they say yes to your solution.

Maybe it's visuals contrasting a cluttered, stressful office to an organized, productive workspace after using your storage systems. Or statistics showing the revenue increase a business witnessed after adopting your software.

Get them to imagine and crave that "after" result for themselves.

### Leverage Powerful Testimonials

Speaking of customer stories, testimonials are perfect for letting your raving fans sell the change for you.

Quotes like "I went from struggling entrepreneur to 6-figure business owner after finding this program" or "This workout plan helped me finally get my dream body" clearly illustrate the change that is possible because someone else has already experienced it.

Go beyond just text. Video testimonials of real customers gleefully describing their transformations can be quite relatable and thus more persuasive via social proof.

### Highlight Impressive Case Studies and Selling to Status

For bigger initiatives or B2B offerings, detailed case studies provide an in-depth look at the remarkable changes your products or services can drive. Once again, this plays into social proof as well as loss aversion—the status quo will become less and less attractive.

Walk through a client's challenges, the solutions you implemented, and the measurable outcomes they achieved as a result.

With a well-crafted case study, you're not just selling a product—you're selling a proven framework for solving their problems and reaching their goals.

"Leaders like you have leveraged…" or "Adopting this tool…" or "This is your opportunity to…" are ways to sell to status.

That's when objections fade because the prospect can start to envision their own success story as part of the overall journey.

## KEY TAKEAWAYS

At the end of the day, reducing fear and anxiety in the buying process is all about building trust, confidence, and clarity for your prospects.

By understanding the deep-rooted psychological factors at play, you can deploy smart tactics like risk-reversal guarantees, social proof, and credibility-boosting content. Perhaps most importantly, however, sell the transformation, not just the product.

When you can vividly show buyers how their lives or businesses will improve after saying "yes," that's when doubts get replaced by excited anticipation for the positive change to come. If worry creeps in again later, remind buyers about the vision once more.

Master these strategies and you'll be closing more sales by neutralizing those objections and fears once and for all. That is, until the next buyer on the committee throws a wrinkle in things…but that's for the next chapter.

# SOUND BYTE SUMMARY

— Without carefully developing the business case, deals have little chance of developing or closing.
— Use the business case to progress deals through cocreation with buyers.
— A great business case is slim but tailored specifically to the buyers and stakeholders on the Buying Committee.
— Sometimes a business case will not have the seller's name nor the seller's company name on it, precisely because it needs to be sold internally.

To get access to all of the templates, frameworks, tools, and podcast episodes referenced in this book, visit this link: **growthforum.io/bonuses**

# NEXT UP

How are you going to consistently and ethically close deals? That depends on how well you understand the Buying Committee. Which strategy will you employ to help the Buying Committee come to a consensus?

CHAPTER 8

# THE BUYING COMMITTEE

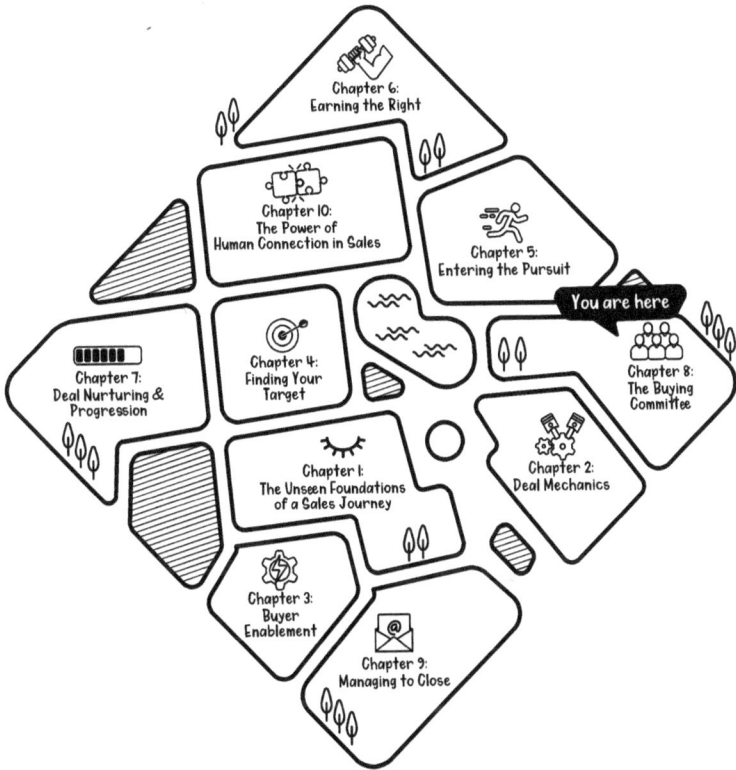

Chapter 6:
Earning the Right

Chapter 10:
The Power of
Human Connection in Sales

Chapter 5:
Entering the Pursuit

You are here

Chapter 7:
Deal Nurturing &
Progression

Chapter 4:
Finding Your
Target

Chapter 8:
The Buying
Committee

Chapter 1:
The Unseen Foundations
of a Sales Journey

Chapter 2:
Deal Mechanics

Chapter 3:
Buyer
Enablement

Chapter 9:
Managing to Close

# The ins and outs of *selling to*
# *a Buying Committee* of any size

F orty to 60 percent of B2B deals end in the dreaded No Decision. Another way of putting it: those buyers decided the cost of inaction was preferred to the pain of change.

Buyers (plural) because the number of people involved in decisions is increasing. If you think there are two decision-makers, there are probably four. If you think there are four, there are probably eight.

We once worked on an enterprise deal with 34 people...

Each decision-maker in the group adds on additional risk because it makes it harder to reach consensus, and B2B buying is already complex.

Jen Allen-Knuth often talks about the impact of No Decision and how to leverage the cost of inaction, which we love.

However, before we can even look at the cost of inaction, we need to determine if you have engaged each stakeholder and delivered what they need.

A great question to ask is: who else should be involved in this decision?

## UNDERSTANDING THE BUYING COMMITTEE

Each buyer has a unique DiSC profile and knowledge matrix.

As the deal progresses, make note of these. How can you best communicate with each? How does your messaging adapt? Remember that mirroring communication styles generally works well, if you don't have a clear plan.

Don't overthink this. When in doubt, use mirroring, yes, but more importantly ensure you are prepared for every interaction and meeting so that you can facilitate the deal progression, overcome objections effectively (from the buyer's perspective), and remain focused on the business case's commercial ROI that comes from actually solving the problem at hand.

If you are using a CRM or even working within a team, notes on communication styles can be kept for each buyer as reminders.

### Cost of Inaction

What happens when the Buying Committee does nothing? If they choose to keep the status quo?

If the Buying Committee fully understood the business case, then generally speaking, this means the Buying Committee chose the cost of inaction over the perceived growing pains of change.

In this case, it is possible to better emphasize the cost of inaction during the process of codeveloping the business case. This way, the choice is between the cost of inaction and the benefit of change—instead of whether to accept your proposed solution or not.

### Challenger Questions

What if we looked at all this from a different perspective?

That's the goal of challenger questions. To jolt awake the buyer to see something from a fresh point of view.

It might simply be done by offering an opinion about the cost of inaction, as described in the prior section, but it could be any number of awareness-raising insights.

In order to help the challenger questions land, it's important to establish familiarity and credibility with the buyer. Language like "Typically, we see this…" can work quite well.

If the buyer clams up a bit or if relationship tension develops, ease up a bit to show you are listening to their body language, then continue once the flow of discussion is resumed.

# NAVIGATING CONFLICT TO REDUCE RELATIONSHIP TENSION

It's always possible for relationship tension and even conflict to arise.

It is a uniquely human skill to navigate such tension or conflict and come out of it even more aligned toward a solution, with the relationship still intact.

I started working for local cafes and restaurants from age 14 to 23 as part-time work. I enjoyed these jobs, as they taught me many soft skills, such as dealing with conflict, building rapport with customers, and general good manners, that would stay with me throughout life.

When customers want something and the expectation is that they get it, and then they don't, they can feel let down.

With coworkers, tension can also arise. So that this friction doesn't affect the customer experience, it is useful to apply the soft skills in these moments.

When there is alignment toward a customer outcome, then the coworkers can agree to work toward that together, putting aside any personal tension that may still be there. Also recognize that tension can build a shared experience that helps people grow.

Listening, acknowledging people, and trying to set things right goes a long way, even if it all started with a small oversight.

## STRATEGIES TO APPROACH THE BUYING COMMITTEE

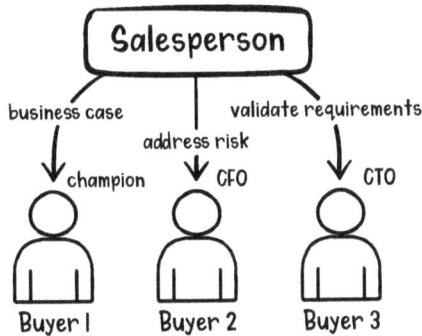

In Chapter 3, Luigi described working with a 34-person Buying Committee, which remains a great relationship to this day.

If the Buying Committee is that large, it is useful to narrow the communication slightly to maintain focus. Generally, there are these key categories of buyers:

- Decision-Maker
- User
- Economic Buyer
- Assassin, the Anti-Sponsor who doesn't want you there
- Champion (or Sponsor)

The **Decision-Maker** is the one (or many) who has a stake in the decision being finalized. They will have to be happy with the business case and how the solution will be implemented. If there are multiple final decision-makers, find out what each needs to progress to the point of decision. For example, the Chief Technology Officer (CTO) will likely need to validate the technical requirements.

**Users** are those whose work lives will be affected by the solution being adopted. Doing discovery with users will help to anticipate aspects of the implementation plan that may have risk.

The **Economic Buyer** is typically the CFO. The CFO will have to do his diligence to ensure the numbers make sense and fit into the company's overall financial position, strategy, and plans.

The **Assassin**, also known as the **Anti-Sponsor**, will typically be countering your progress for a variety of reasons, whether political, economic, or personal. Instead of antagonizing the Assassin, jujitsu can be performed to turn the other cheek and use the Assassin's negativity and objections to further educate the Champion and those eager to see the deal progress. It's as important to listen to the Assassin as it is to the Champion.

The **Champion** (or Sponsor) is likely your biggest internal resource in terms of building momentum for the solution you are helping to bring to the company.

Sorting out how to approach all these buyers takes some thought and planning. (There will be a bit more about each of these buyers in the Marketing section of this chapter, called segmented messaging strategy.)

Where is the company in their buying process? What do you know about previous buying cycles? Were you involved? Or do you know someone who was on either the sales or buying side?

As a starting point, it can be good to keep the answers to these questions in your Buyer Personas or in your CRM under those contacts or deals.

## Multiple Champions

The fact is that many deals require more than one champion: that is, multiple buyers who are actively supporting your solution.

Some sellers prefer to stick with one champion because it streamlines communication.

But if more than one buyer is engaged in promoting the business case that you've codeveloped internally, that means more voices and more internal touches are being made. This keeps the solution you've brought in people's daily awareness.

And when it comes to key decisions, whether for budget or otherwise, there will be an extra vote in your favor as well.

When bringing on a second or third champion, be sure to involve the original champion so that there isn't unnecessary relationship tension created. Know the personal metrics of each champion and their motivations for getting this deal on the table internally. Then make it a win-win for both.

Each stakeholder (including the champions) hears and values things differently. In fact, in some cases, each stakeholder also has conflicting priorities with their colleagues.

This is why it's important to have a clear understanding of the different stakeholders in the Buying Committee before seeking to progress an opportunity.

Ask your champion:

- What level of priority does this project have with…?
- How important is it for them that this project is executed?
- What other projects could this impact?
- What risks and concerns might they have about…?

Without understanding this, you cannot then enable your champion to navigate the next steps.

Your message must speak to all the decision-makers (or have varying messages to each), or else the likelihood of No Decision increases.

It may seem like you can never fully understand every player or stakeholder in a given Buying Committee, but inevitably your approach can shift to make this your goal.

## Checkpoint 8:
## What Other Projects Could This Impact?

*Just as there are checkpoints in a sales and buying journey, there will be checkpoints through this book to test your learning and application: learning without application is simply entertainment.*

### Expanding the Thinking of Your Buyers

*The idea of asking questions like "What other projects could this impact?" is—we argue—a necessary kind of question, not only to show you care, but also to expand the thinking of the buyer. Your pragmatic research, discovery, and engagement with this buyer and buyers in the same field may give you the confidence to already know the answer, but it's still critical to ask. Leave no stone unturned! Buyers expect this level of investment and genuine care, and it's possible your assumptions may be wrong! A great chance to humble yourself and always be learning.*

## Who to Talk to First

Stepping back to your first engagement with a company or set of prospects...who should you talk to first?

This depends on the type of organization as well as what you prefer to do. We have had a lot of success approaching the mid-level in a larger organization, developing a relationship, and then working with that champion to get endorsement for the deal.

But often, the salesperson goes to the decision-maker straight away. This is logical because that person will ultimately decide.

But what if this person relies on input from several, or many, others? If you haven't looped in those stakeholders in the right way, you might not be getting your endorsement if you've leap-frogged them. And if they haven't been educated—if they are pre-awareness or early awareness—then it will take a bit of work to provide that education here.

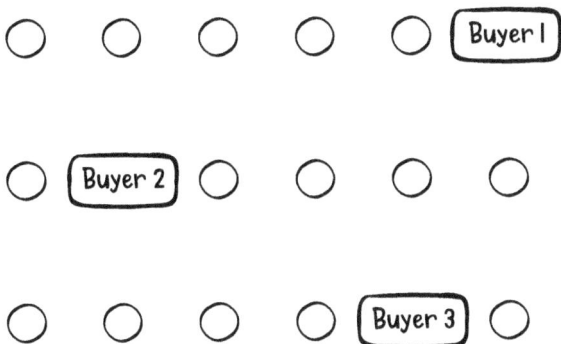

If you recognize that you've gone too far ahead with one buyer in real time without bringing along the others, try to reduce relationship tension by explaining how you plan to engage those other buyers before returning to provide value to the decision-maker. Then, deliver on this promise.

Another strategy, instead of approaching key decision-makers or mid-level stakeholders seeking a champion, is to start with the other end of the spectrum by going to users.

This way you can learn from the bottom up so to speak with respect to the problem space. Even if you feel you've already done enough discovery, asking questions in user conversations gives you additional confidence and validation and also provides a track record of conversations you can build upon. "When I met with

NAME, she helped me understand THIS, which makes me better able to provide THIS insight."

Whatever place you start, eventually you are going to *find your Champion.* This is the one who will "champion" the idea throughout the buying process. There's something they like about what you've brought, whether it's your point of view, the way you've provided value upfront, or maybe simply your level of sales professionalism… and there's something they have started to sense in the process of learning about solutions you've brought to their attention.

Learn and understand the Champion's motivations and you will be able to give them what they need to be successful selling internally, with you just doing the right amount of facilitation, not too little, not too much.

Be sure to gauge the Champion's level of understanding about how to sell within their organization so that this can be facilitated as well.

## SEGMENTED MESSAGING STRATEGY

Imagine you're at a party with a Chief Executive Officer (CEO), an intern, and a bartender, and you want to start a conversation with each of them. You might approach the CEO with a different topic than the intern and have a different tone with the bartender. Everyone has their own perspective and interests, so the same conversation starter can't work for everyone.

The same goes for your B2B marketing messages, especially when you're trying to close a deal with a Buying Committee. A segmented messaging strategy is what assigns "Good day! I heard about your company" to the CEO, "Hi there! How is your internship experience so far?" to the intern, and "Hey there! People are saying that you make the best cocktails in town!" to the bartender.

So who's who in the Buying Committee? What exactly is a segmented messaging strategy? How can it help you close deals more effectively?

## Crafting the Perfect Message for the Buying Committee

Unlike B2C marketing, which aims to dazzle individual customers, B2B marketing has to cater to multiple layers of interests, concerns, and needs. In the B2B world, the stakes can be high, and a group of people—the Buying Committee we've been chatting about—make the decisions.

Simply put, a segmented messaging strategy is all about tailoring your communication to speak directly to each key player within the Buying Committee. Think of it as tailoring a custom suit—you choose each stitch, pattern, and fabric with care to fit perfectly. How do you do that?

### The Decision-Maker

Let's talk about the key Decision-Makers. Think CEO, Chief Operating Officer (COO), or the president of a company. When talking to them, highlight strategic benefits and showcase technical prowess.

Meanwhile, your go-to guy or gal for all things tech could be the CTO, CIO, or IT manager. These people will scrutinize the technical aspects, integration capabilities, and security features.

If the COO or operations manager is involved, they will want to know about keeping the wheels turning by focusing on efficiency, process improvement, and resource management.

### The Users

The Users are those who'll be using your solution day in and day out. They'll give you the lowdown on what works and what doesn't in their current routine. Speak to their pain points and how your solution makes their job easier, freeing up time for what really matters.

Think about designers, marketers, and content creators, too. These individuals thrive on creativity and innovation. Try sparking their interest with "What if you could channel all your creative energy without getting bogged down by mundane tasks? Our tool lets you focus on creating magic while we handle the details."

### The Economic Buyer

The Economic Buyer is the company's Money Maestro. Usually, this is your CFO. They're all about the dollars and cents and ensuring everything financially aligns with the company's big picture. Instead of bogging them down with technical jargon, highlight cost savings, ROI, and long-term financial benefits, provide hard numbers!

Economic Buyers are always on the lookout for cost-effective solutions that bring significant value to their companies. Address their focus on ROI with a message like "What if you could achieve more with less? Our solution offers exceptional value by streamlining processes and reducing overhead costs, making you spend every penny of your budget well."

CFOs also play a significant role in mitigating risks and achieving financial stability. Cater to their cautious nature with "Imagine having the confidence that solid data and risk assessments back every financial decision you make. Our solution minimizes uncertainties and maximizes stability, providing a dependable foundation for your financial strategies."

### The Assassin

Meet the Assassin, sometimes known as the Anti-Sponsor, who might be throwing a wrench in your plans for various reasons—political, economic, or personal. Rather than butting heads, flip the script on their negativity and objections and provide evidence to counter them. "I'm glad you asked!" Use their feedback to improve your pitch and demonstrate your solution's resilience.

For example, an analyst needs concrete data to be persuaded. Provide them with extensive, transparent data to prove your solution's effectiveness: "Check out our comprehensive metrics and case studies proving our solution's consistent success and ROI. See how investing in our solution has yielded measurable improvements for similar companies!"

Individuals loyal to legacy systems may also resist new implementations due to comfort with existing processes. Address their comfort with "Our solution not only coexists with but enhances your current systems."

### The Champion

Lastly, the Champion or Sponsor is like a secret weapon on your team. They're your biggest internal ally, helping build excitement and momentum for the fantastic solution you're bringing to the table. As such, provide them with tools, data, and success stories to champion your cause. Keep them in the loop and support their efforts.

On the one hand, there are the strategic visionaries who are always looking at the bigger picture and future-proofing their organization. Empower them with insights that align with their forward-thinking mindset: "By integrating our solution, you'll be positioning your company at the forefront of innovation. Our track record shows how organizations like yours stay ahead of industry trends and continuously evolve to meet future challenges."

On the other hand, change advocates thrive on transformation and improvement within the organization. Encourage their support with cultural and performance impact messages: "Implementing our solution will drive a culture of continuous improvement and adaptability. Let us lead you to greater overall success and employee satisfaction."

## Segmented Messaging in Action

The Buying Committee isn't a figment of the imagination; it's a group of real people with individual motivations and goals. A segmented messaging strategy isn't there to trick them; you design them to deliver tailored, motivating content to the right person.

It takes effort and tools to bring people together to make a decision. If you really want to seal the deal, use these said resources to their full potential. Let's look at an example of how a segmented messaging strategy can lead to a successful deal closure.

A buzzing tech company is in the market for a new project management tool. The Buying Committee consists of three key players:

- Jane, a forward-thinking CTO,
- Sam, the practical HR Manager, and
- Claire, the enthusiastic Head of Innovation

Jane is all about future-proofing the company, so the tech company hits her with insights on how the tool integrates the latest AI advancements to streamline workflow and predict project outcomes. Jane will be thrilled with the idea of staying ahead of the curve and driving technological innovation.

Meanwhile, Sam needs something that improves team productivity without adding complexity. The tech company can send him a detailed case study showing how the user-friendly interface cut onboarding time by half, resulting in a 20% increase in employee efficiency. Consequently, he'll be sold by the prospect of such tangible improvements.

Let's not forget Claire, who thrives on transforming ideas into action. To her, the tech company emphasizes the cultural shift the tool brings—encouraging collaboration and creative problem-solving. When she reads about the cultural impact and how it leads to a fun, dynamic workplace, she'll be ready to champion the solution.

When the Buying Committee members regroup, they will be on board and sing praises from different angles. This cohesive yet segmented approach captures their unique needs and ultimately seals the deal by getting all the buyers to buy in.

## Bringing It All Together

Let's be clear about one thing: segmented messaging is not just about closing the deal; it's about creating a win-win situation for everyone involved. It always requires thorough research, strategic planning, and, most importantly, effective communication.

The next time you're at that metaphorical party, remember—one size doesn't fit all. Consider each guest carefully and tell them the things they want to hear.

For the Decision Maker, emphasize how your solution aligns with the company's long-term goals and provide detailed technical specs, case studies, and future scalability. For the User, address daily challenges and demonstrate ease of use.

For the Economic Buyer, focus on financial impact. When dealing with the Assassin, acknowledge concerns and engage constructively. Lastly, with the Champion, empower your advocate and maintain close communication.

The result? Everyone says yes, and you get to leave the party with new friends (or clients).

## SOUND BYTE SUMMARY

— Approach the Buying Committee strategically by developing a plan to approach each buyer at the right time with the right information, tailored to them.
— Learn what each buyer's questions are so that you can be proactive in providing value to preempt objections
— Work with the Champion (or Champions) to develop the business case and validate it internally
— No Decision is your biggest competitor.

> To get access to all of the templates, frameworks, tools, and podcast episodes referenced in this book, visit this link: **growthforum.io/bonuses**

## NEXT UP

Closing time. But even when you close, the work isn't done...

# MANAGING TO CLOSE

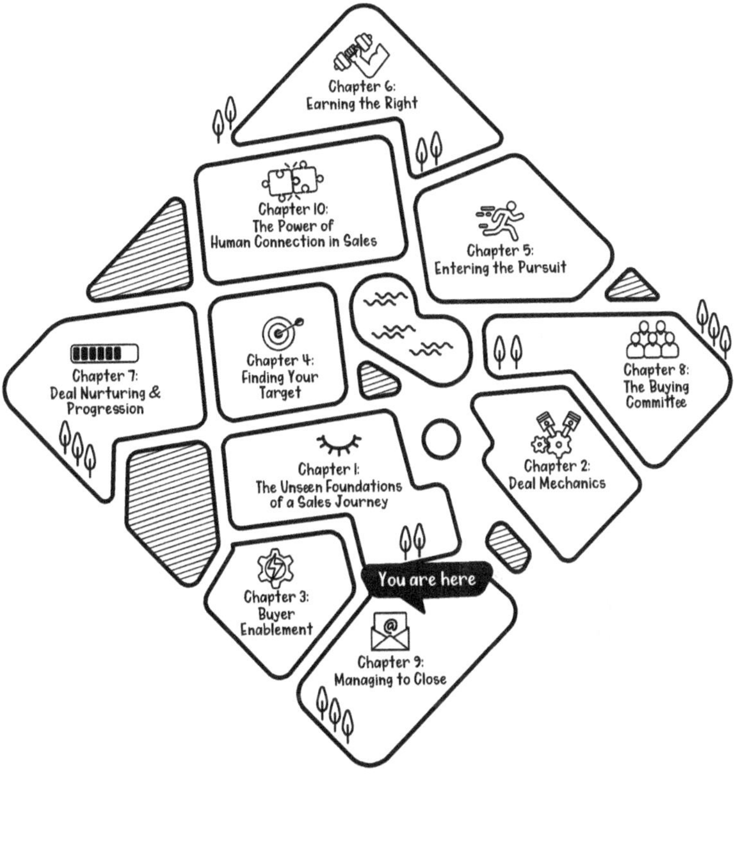

Chapter 6:
Earning the Right

Chapter 10:
The Power of
Human Connection in Sales

Chapter 5:
Entering the Pursuit

Chapter 7:
Deal Nurturing &
Progression

Chapter 4:
Finding Your
Target

Chapter 8:
The Buying
Committee

Chapter 1:
The Unseen Foundations
of a Sales Journey

Chapter 2:
Deal Mechanics

Chapter 3:
Buyer
Enablement

You are here

Chapter 9:
Managing to Close

Notice your own fear of rejection, then spot the difference between objections, stalls, and conditions in the latter stages of a deal so that you can *manage to close* within your offer process, tying into the buying journey.

"Harvey Spectre is the best closer this city has ever seen."
If you ever watched the television show *Suits*, you would think you were watching a bunch of smooth-talking salespeople negotiating and closing deals. Somehow they seem to always get their buyers to say, "This absolutely makes sense for us."

However, when it comes to selling, the actual philosophy is completely the opposite. Closing occurs *before* you start the sale. It's not some mythical part of the process where you are able to CLOSE the deal with various closing techniques.

Yes, certain techniques can enable you to stimulate buyers to take action. However, in B2B sales, where multiple people are involved in the buying process, using outdated closing techniques can often kill the deal instead of progressing it. Remember your role in the process is to facilitate, guide, and nurture. You are bringing a team together and ensuring there is alignment and consensus.

Even Harvey was constantly asking his sidekick Mike Ross to do research and other work to assist him. Whether you're going solo or part of a team of salespeople, that necessary work can't be skipped.

This is where the process will become your best friend. It helps you prepare in the right way for the key moments and consistently deliver value. The way in which you manage the process will often impact your close and win rate. All too often, I hear salespeople tell me why following all the steps creates too much administration and takes too much time.

What are the consequences of not leveraging the tools and following the process? Deals can take longer to close, start to stall, and require extra follow-up to try to engage the buyer again.

Let's look at a great example of how following the process can shorten deal cycles.

I have worked with a large global payment provider for a number of years. The team worked on large enterprise deals. The average close time was over 300 days.

When we first introduced the Sales OS process to the team, we were met with fierce resistance: "We don't have the time; we already have to spend time updating the CRM." After the initial reactions, once the team was able to see things from a different perspective, they tried the process. Fast-forward twelve months, and the average time to close a deal was shortened to just over 100 days.

## The Offer Process (Reminder)

Let's pause and remember what we discussed previously to understand where the offer process fits in. It's critical to follow the steps not only of the overall buying journey but within a sales process that fits into that buyer journey.

Within the offer process, there are 6 points:

1. Set the Agenda—Set the scene
2. Current State—Confirm situation is still current
3. Future State—Ensure future state goal is still relevant
4. How—I know the product but don't know you
5. Investment—Ready to buy
6. Next steps—Set the action plan

Staying true to this process ensures you don't skip any steps and can facilitate confidently.

What's interesting is the close doesn't just create tension for buyers. It can also create tension for sellers.

If we can dissipate the tension, keep the buyer(s) on the path to a confident decision, and get them to say, "This absolutely makes sense for us," then we have truly managed to close.

Let's start with the tension you may be feeling in the role of facilitator.

## FACILITATOR TENSION

When a salesperson attempts to close a deal, several psychological and neurological processes occur in the brain, often driven by a mix of **reward anticipation, fear response,** and **cognitive dissonance.** Here's what's happening at a deeper level:

### 1. Anticipation of Reward (Dopamine Release)

The brain's dopamine system plays a key role during the closing stage of a sale. Dopamine, often referred to as the "feel-good" neurotransmitter, is released in anticipation of a reward (e.g., closing the deal). It triggers excitement and motivates the salesperson to push forward.

However, the anticipation can also create a heightened emotional state, making the salesperson anxious about achieving the desired outcome.

### 2. Activation of the Fight-or-Flight Response (Amygdala Activation)

The amygdala, a part of the brain associated with processing emotions and threats, can become active during the closing stage. The brain may perceive the risk of rejection or failure as a threat, triggering the fight-or-flight response.

This response releases cortisol, the stress hormone, which can cause symptoms of anxiety like increased heart rate, shallow breathing, and nervousness. The brain shifts focus to potential risks, making the salesperson more sensitive to signs of objection or hesitation from the prospect.

### 3. Cognitive Dissonance

Salespeople might experience **cognitive dissonance** when there is a conflict between their belief in the value of the product and their fear of rejection. The discomfort arises because the salesperson is trying to maintain confidence while simultaneously fearing a negative outcome.

To resolve this tension, the brain seeks to align beliefs and actions. This is why experienced salespeople often use self-affirmation or reframe the situation as a chance to help the prospect rather than simply closing a deal.

### 4. The Fear of Loss (Loss Aversion)

Loss aversion, a principle from behavioral economics, is a powerful psychological phenomenon during closing. The human brain is wired to fear losses more than it values equivalent gains. For the salesperson, the potential loss of a deal (and associated commission, recognition, or success) feels more significant than the potential gain.

This fear of loss can cause hesitation or even self-sabotage, where the salesperson may avoid asking for the close directly or become overly cautious.

## ARRIVING AT A POINT OF DECISION

When buyers or a team of buyers move to a point of decision, anxiety can often kick in related to the above points. Usually it relates to low energy states like apathy or fear. Task tension will rise.

When a decision is required, emotions arise. Why? Because now the conversation about what is possible and the work needed to get there becomes a reality.

And often, buyers start freaking out about their ability to manage the project.

This uneasiness is what often kills deals. Status quo bias weighs on the buyer's mind, and the committee starts to wonder if the pain of change is greater than the **pain of same**. They may reason that the status quo isn't great, but at least it is familiar.

So the buyer softens and does nothing.

This is where the skill of managing resistance will become so important in helping buyers and the Buying Committee, especially in B2B sales, through the final step of the process.

However, before tackling this, we have to first understand why objections trigger emotion and can lead us to react.

You spend all this time managing a deal and meeting multiple people, working on a scoping brief, and developing a business case. You can see the finish line; the deal is ready to close, and you start to think about that commission that will come, even though that's not what drives you.

But you do think about it. And you may even spend part of it…

Then, all of a sudden, you sense the committee has concerns. They share some feedback about the project, and a knot forms in your stomach.

Anxiety starts to kick in not only for them but for you. We fear objections because we…

- Fear rejection,
- Lack preparation,
- Experience uncertainty,
- Are conflict-avoidant, or
- Perceive an imminent failure.

So, to truly develop the skill to help buyers work through objections, we must first work on our emotional state and how we manage the emotional stress this part of the process can create for us as the salesperson.

Here, we need to ask questions. Illicit to get more information. To work with them and walk them through it.

As a result of the anxiety and emotional stress, bottom-of-the-funnel objections need to be handled very carefully. If they aren't, the deal could stall or be lost. Remember: an objection is a request for more information before I buy.

As a seller, you may feel the urgency to move to a decision. But we need to make *sure* we have ***permission to move to the next step.***

Also, be aware of the hidden objections. We need to address buyers' true concerns.

## TASK TENSION
## AND MANAGING RESISTANCE

| Stall | Terms/Conditions | True Objection |

Thinking back to previous stages of the deal, you led with value, shared insights, and educated prospects. They've even come to see you as a trusted partner. Now, see it through to the end—close with conviction by listening for tension at the bottom of the funnel.

When buyers move to a point of decision, task tension often kicks in. Emotions start to drive their decision. They start to realize that they are now at a point of turning a concept into a reality. They question themselves and their team.

This is why we need to carefully massage and manage the process.

## Top of Funnel vs. Bottom of Funnel Resistance

Resistance at the top of the funnel is different to resistance at the bottom of the funnel. The top of the funnel is often relationship focused. At the bottom of the funnel, the time has passed, and the opportunity is qualified. Multiple stakeholders are engaged. Now, we are moving the conversation to a point of decision.

We've touched on objections in previous chapters, including reducing fear and anxiety in Chapter 7 and navigating the needs of different players on the Buying Committee in Chapter 8. Already in this chapter we've talked about **task tension**.

It's true that questions will arise at each stage of the deal; however, in managing to close, all those objections that have been unanswered and any new objections definitely need to be overcome if the deal is going to close and the solution implemented.

First, one useful definition of an objection is *a request for more information before I move forward.*

A spoken objection is an information gap expressed in words.

### Presenting Your Proposal Live

What's the difference between sending your proposal versus actually presenting your proposal? The consequence when sending proposals is that deals can ghost you. They can go from hot to cold literally within hours.

Why? Because when buyers read a proposal, they will have questions. And if you are not there to help answer those questions, they will often answer them themselves. And in most cases, they aren't answering those questions correctly. When they misinterpret, the deal dies.

But when you are there to field their questions, to ask clarifying questions, and to listen to concerns, facilitating the next step is much smoother.

Whatever is said aloud, often the true objection is below the surface.

Buyers, if they don't have answers, based on their assessment and assumptions, *will come up with their own answers.*

That's why it's important to elicit responses and concerns. Because if left to simmer, the objection lingers and blocks a deal from moving ahead.

Again, an objection is *I need to know xx before progressing...*

- Do you want them to come up with that answer for themselves?
- Eventually, the justification is "This isn't a priority right now."

There are fears and unanswered questions. But information gaps can be filled in:

- These are some of the challenges
- These are some of the steps
- If you do this, you can tap into this audience (business case validation)
- Investing to capture the market

The outcome to get to → "This absolutely makes sense for us."

> ## Checkpoint 9:
> ## A Request for More Information
>
> *Just as there are checkpoints in a sales and buying journey, there will be checkpoints through this book to test your learning and application: learning without application is simply entertainment.*
>
> ### Maintaining Progress Toward Confident Decisions
>
> *We know the outcome is "This absolutely makes sense for us."*
>
> *But the reality is there was probably a recent deal where this didn't happen. Examine the interactions with the buyer and Buying Committee. Can you pinpoint where there was a chance to give information that was missed? Can you add a clear step within the Alignment (Collaboration) stage to ensure that information is asked for and given?*

## FEAR OF REJECTION

In our line of work, there are two words you often hear from customers that can mean success or failure.

These words are "yes" and (the dreaded) "no."

As a sales pro or start-up owner, you've likely had more of the latter than the former. With this being the case, you may have developed a fear of rejection.

Yes, rejection is a real thing in sales and business.

Sometimes, we fear objections because of fear of rejection.

*The rejections you've faced may not have been rejections.*

Read that again if you have to.

Often, we get too sensitive when we get a "no."

This causes us to overgeneralize the experience and label it as a sign to back off.

With the right sales mindset, you'll experience a paradigm shift in how you think of rejections. You'll reframe what you thought were rejections into the very things you get out of bed for—opportunities.

### All About Rejection

Hearing a "no," experiencing rejection, doesn't have to be the stuff of nightmares.

Simply put, rejections are any correspondence or behavior that signifies that your customer isn't interested in what you're selling. Rejections during top-of-funnel activities are one thing, but at the bottom of the funnel, this can spark many emotions.

As a result, rejections can strike fear and despair in even the staunchest and "Goggins-esque" of sales pros.

If you're nodding your head to this, you're no less a person or a salesperson.

In fact, it's possible we're hard-wired to fear rejection. At the same time, failure provides a continuous learning process, which is to call back to Chapter 1 on Mindset.

### Objection—Opportunities Masked as Rejection

We're taught that rejection sucks and is a sign to back off.

But what if it isn't?

Think of the last time you got a "rejection."

Did the exchange look like this?

You pitched a product.

The prospect showed some interest but, for some reason, didn't bite.

Instead, your customer told you things along the lines of:
"I like it. But it's too (insert reason)."

**Sure, the outcome looks the same as a rejection—this is the number one mistake most sales professionals make.**

You see, the above exchange isn't a rejection.

Why?

It's because, unlike a rejection, *your prospect showed interest.*

They said, "I like it, but..."

What stopped your prospect or lead from buying was a specific factor. Whatever this factor is, that's a sales objection.

**Objections are requests for more information before progressing.**

Think of them as signals that your prospect is engaged and interested but may have concerns or questions holding them back, like a hiker at a fork in the mountain path, reading the signage to decide which to take. Be the guide.

## Spotting Sales Objections

Recognizing objections is crucial for effective sales conversations.

They can come in many forms, such as:

**Stall:** "I don't want to make a decision right now."
**Price:** "It's too expensive."
**Value:** "I'm not seeing the benefit of what is being presented."
**Trust:** "I'm not confident that we can implement this."
**Concern:** "We're keen, but we have a few concerns."

These objections may seem like barriers, but with the right sales mindset and approach, they can be transformed into opportunities.

Bear in mind that often, the true objection sits beneath common objections like price, timing, need, or competition. Like an iceberg, the true objection is often hidden underwater.

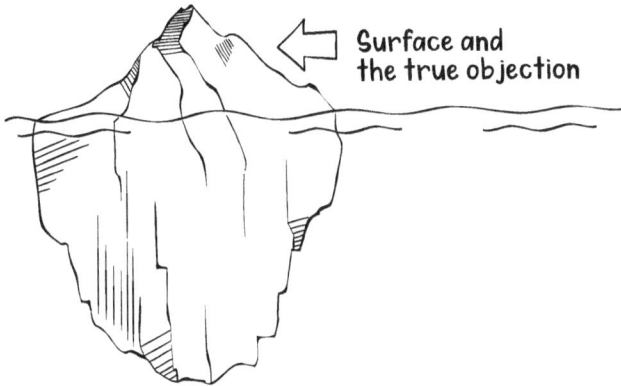

Surface and the true objection

They're learning opportunities that tell you more about your customers.

Most importantly, they enable you to get to the bottom of what makes a sale challenging by asking, listening, and learning—then you can address it.

## HELP BUYERS MANAGE RESISTANCE: THE PLAYBOOK

If you've made it this far, we can sum up everything that has been said like this:

See rejections as unrecognized objections.
Spot objections.
Address them.

As salespeople, we should know the most common barriers that often hinder a deal from moving forward. So, instead of using hope as a strategy, lean into objections. Be the one to raise them first.

Reference how others feel like xx during a certain stage of the process. This will often lead the prospect to agree and show they are also feeling a form of anxiety about a particular topic.

Here's a hack: If you struggle with this, then review your last five deals that stalled or did not move forward. Determine the objection. This will allow you to develop a trend of the objections and barriers that stopped the deal from progressing. Then your strategy is to develop a message that will talk to the concern or objection the prospect is sharing.

We also need to talk about reducing relationship tension. That's when barriers occur. We don't fight them. We don't argue. We mirror.

### How Mirroring Works

- **Psychological Connection:** When you mirror someone's words, they subconsciously feel more understood and validated. This makes them more likely to open up and continue the conversation. It signals attentiveness without appearing confrontational or demanding.
- **Encourages the Other Person to Elaborate:** Mirroring encourages the other person to explain their thoughts in more detail. By reflecting their words back to them, you prompt them to dive deeper into what they're saying without feeling pressured.

- **Lowers Relationship Tension:** Mirroring reduces relationship tension by creating a feeling of comfort. When people hear their own words repeated back to them, they feel acknowledged and are less likely to become defensive. This technique fosters a smoother dialogue, which is critical in high-stakes negotiations where emotions might be heightened.

Mirroring is a far better strategy than fighting the objection, refusing to listen to what is being shared, responding immediately, showing emotion or confusion, or conveying your disappointment.

## Addressing Objections

So far, we've talked about seeing rejections as unrecognized objections and how to spot them.

So how do you go about addressing them?

Here's our step-by-step plan for dealing with objections, overcoming them, and nailing your sales conversations:

1. Listen Actively
2. Empathize
3. Clarify and Confirm
4. Provide Solutions
5. Handle Objections Proactively
6. Reduce Cognitive Dissonance

Let's take them one by one.

### 1. Listen Actively

Active listening is the foundation of effective objection handling.

Rather than immediately jumping in with a response, take the time to understand the prospect's objection fully.

Listen not just to the words they're saying but also to the underlying concerns and emotions behind the objection.

This demonstrates to the prospect that you value their perspective and are genuinely interested in finding a solution that meets their needs.

Of course, it's one thing just to listen—it's another to display that you're attentive, and this is what you want to do to put your prospect at ease.

To display your attentiveness, simply use open body language (don't cross your arms) and rephrase or restate based on what you understood.

Doing these two things goes a long way.

### 2. Empathize

Empathy is essential in building rapport and trust with prospects.

Put yourself in the prospect's shoes and acknowledge their concerns with sincerity.

Use phrases like "I understand how you feel" or "That sounds challenging" to show empathy and validate their emotions.

While doing this, slow down the pace. This lowers the relationship tension and allows you to mirror the buyer.

By demonstrating empathy, you create a connection with the prospect and create a more conducive environment for addressing their objections.

Listening and taking these objections in stride also makes you seem less "salesy" or "too pushy," which can be quite off-putting to your customers.

### 3. Clarify and Confirm

Ensure that you fully understand the prospect's objection before attempting to address it.

Ask clarifying questions to gain a deeper understanding of their concerns.

Repeat the objection back to the prospect in your own words to confirm your understanding and show that you're actively engaged.

This not only helps clarify any misunderstandings but also demonstrates to the prospect that you're genuinely listening and attentive to their needs.

## 4. Provide Solutions

At the end of the day, sales objections are pain points or problems.

Your job as a sales pro is to address them.

Once you've clarified your prospect's objections, focus on providing solutions or alternatives.

Highlight the specific features or benefits of your product or service that directly alleviate their objections.

Tailor your response to resonate with the prospect's needs and pain points.

Last but not least, demonstrate how your offering can effectively solve their problem.

If you can, provide real-world examples or case studies to illustrate the effectiveness of your solution and build credibility.

If you are nearing the point of decision, keep in mind that the Buying Committee is going to need the business case to drive their final decision.

## 5. Handle Objections Proactively

Over time, you'll get a sense of what the most common sales objections are.

Use them as information for future sales pitches.

Anticipating objections before they arise is a proactive approach to objection handling.

Consider common objections that prospects might have. These can be based on their industry, role, or previous interactions. Also, address these objections preemptively during your sales pitch. (Use your ICP and Buyer Personas to track these.)

Work the proactive objections into your presentation and demonstrate how your offering addresses each concern.

This way, you can instil confidence in the prospect and preemptively overcome potential hesitations.

### 6. Reduce Cognitive Dissonance

After a purchase, buyers may experience cognitive dissonance or buyer's remorse. To prevent this, reinforcing the positive aspects of the purchase and reaffirming its value can help to resolve this internal conflict and solidify satisfaction.

### *Example of Cognitive Dissonance*

A decision-maker at a midsized company just signed a contract for a new marketing automation platform. Initially, they were excited about the potential time savings and advanced analytics the platform promised.

However, shortly after signing, they experienced doubts. They begin to wonder...

1. Did they rush into the decision without properly evaluating other options?
2. Will the team adapt well to the new tool, or will there be resistance?
3. Was the investment worth it?

How can we mitigate this cognitive dissonance?

Think about the time from contract execution to project commencement. Reduce this time as much as possible so momentum isn't lost. Time to value is critical. Find ways to drive quick wins.

## Managing Resistance in Action

**Prospect:** "I just don't have the time to take on something new right now. We're really busy."

### 1. Listen Actively—DON'T RESPOND
You pause and show you're listening carefully without jumping in too quickly.

### 2. Empathize
**You:** "Thanks for sharing. I completely understand that finding time for this can be quite challenging."

### 3. Clarify and Confirm
**You:** "Do you mind me asking—outside of time, what other concerns do you have about the project?"

   **Prospect:** "Well, honestly, it's not just time. I'm also worried that our team might not have the capacity to handle the rollout. We're already stretched pretty thin."

### 4. Provide Solutions
**You:** "Thanks for being open about that. I can definitely see how bandwidth would be a concern, especially with a busy team. What's worked really well for other clients in similar situations is our phased implementation process. We break it down into manageable steps so your team can continue with their regular workload without feeling overwhelmed. Plus, many have found that once it's in place, it actually frees up time by automating some of the more repetitive tasks."

## Nothing More Freeing

So there you have it—our approach to overcoming rejection and sales objections.

With a sales mindset that views rejection as objections waiting to be addressed, you'll not just close more, but you'll do so with confidence as though rejection isn't a thing.

And there's nothing more freeing than making deals without the chance of rejection ruling your actions.

It can be a bit of a dance. Enjoy it.

## ETHICAL CLOSING

Do you say whatever you need to get the deal done?

To paraphrase Jeffrey Gitomer, the king of sales: "A sale happens once. A customer buys again and again."

Yet, for some reason, many transactions occur because the seller says whatever they need to close the deal and to close it fast.

They tell the buyer what they want to hear, not necessarily what they don't want to hear.

Because they want the transaction, instead of a relationship.

Picture this: You're in the middle of a deal, meeting multiple stakeholders. During the sales process, you determine a risk. You realize the buyer might not be able to implement what you're proposing.

What do you do? Push the deal forward and ignore the risk?

One could argue that the salesperson's job is to sell, not worry if the buyer gets value from the solution.

However, what would a trusted advisor do?

Larry Levine talks about the importance of trust in the sales process and that selling with love is built around caring and really wanting your buyers to win.

If there's a risk that can be addressed upfront but ignored, is that really caring?

This is a challenge and also a great opportunity for sellers.

When you approach a deal with total transparency, honesty, and sometimes tell your buyer what they don't want to hear, it can create long-term relationships for your relationship funnel that will deliver a far greater return than that one deal.

The real question is…

**Are you prepared to lose a transaction now to gain a long-term relationship?**

We think of it this way: the best salespeople don't sell.

They diagnose.

They listen.

They empathize.

They don't use hacks.

They don't manipulate.

They don't deceive.

They sell ethically.

But the thing is:

- Ethical selling takes more effort
- Ethical selling takes more time

It's easier to pitch a one-size-fits-all solution and trick someone into buying something they don't need.

But the best salespeople know that's not ethical. They know that's not sustainable. They know that's not how you build a long-term sales process.

So, if you want to be a great salesperson, focus on ethical selling.

Build relationships with your clients. Listen to their needs. Empathize with their problems.

That's how you win their trust.

And that's how you close more deals in the long run.

There's a saying: your reputation precedes you.

## DELIVERING AS PROMISED, OR OVERDELIVERING

Everyone knows it's unwise to overpromise and underdeliver.

The opposite is preferred.

If the implementation plan carries too much risk, the deal may be unlikely to get done in the first place. But even a straightforward implementation after the deal closing better get done right.

Nothing tarnishes a reputation faster than undelivered goods that were promised.

If you are truly thinking about the people—the human connections —within the deals you close, then intuitively, the hurdles to implementation will be seen in advance. These will be part of the discussion and built into proposals, accounted for in the business case, and be in writing as part of the delivery plan.

## SOUND BYTE SUMMARY

— An objection is a request for more information before the buyer will move forward.

— Not acknowledging objections allows the buyer to come up with their own (often incorrect) answers to their unanswered questions.

— Handling objections helps you get to "This absolutely makes sense for us."

> To get access to all of the templates, frameworks, tools, and podcast episodes referenced in this book, visit this link:
> **growthforum.io/bonuses**

## NEXT UP

Sales is about helping...people! Learn how to develop truly meaningful relationships where the human connection leads to great business outcomes.

# THE POWER OF HUMAN CONNECTION IN SALES

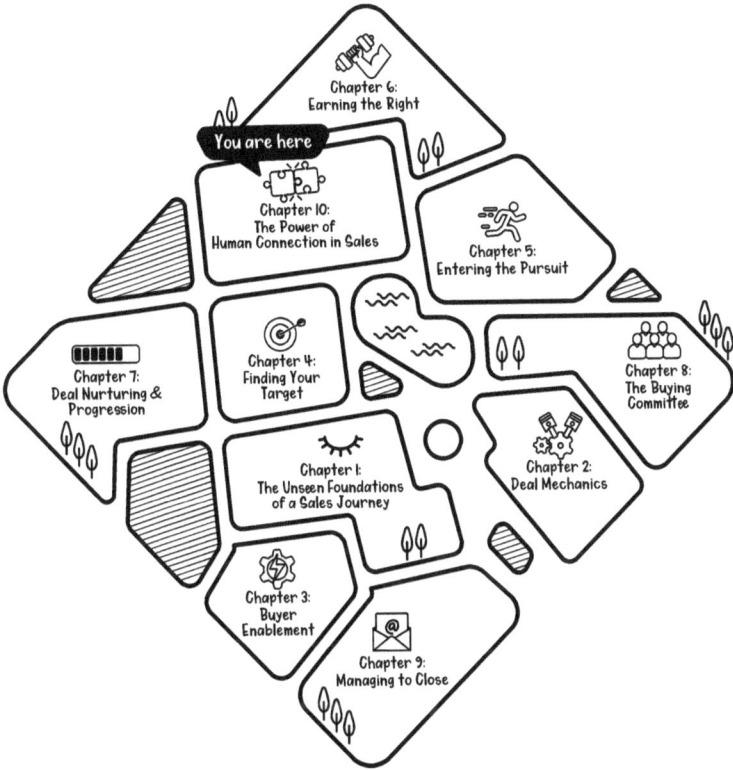

Chapter 6:
Earning the Right

You are here

Chapter 10:
The Power of
Human Connection in Sales

Chapter 5:
Entering the Pursuit

Chapter 7:
Deal Nurturing &
Progression

Chapter 4:
Finding Your
Target

Chapter 8:
The Buying
Committee

Chapter 1:
The Unseen Foundations
of a Sales Journey

Chapter 2:
Deal Mechanics

Chapter 3:
Buyer
Enablement

Chapter 9:
Managing to Close

No matter how many tools become available, **the power of human connection** will always matter in sales because of the lasting outcomes and long-term relationships such connections create.

Sales is an ancient human activity that is thriving today. It's a beautiful, exciting, amazing kind of work. An infinite game connecting those who need help with a path to change.

Focusing on people dissolves the questions about which tools and tech to use. Ask: does this tool or tech help me build trust? That can be the litmus test to decide whether to use it or not in your operating system.

Because people buy from people, a top priority for salespeople everywhere is and should be building and maintaining excellent client relationships.

People not only buy from people, *they buy from people they trust.*

One of the biggest ways to build justified trust is to give value, demonstrating competence and integrity.

That's why when Lui is in sales mode, he prospects every day.

What's the worst possible outcome that could happen from a cold call?

They hang up.

Even that's okay. You wanted to help them and maybe they weren't hearing what you had to say.

We are selling to humans. We are engaging with people. Giving value.

That's why building rapport works by providing insights. It's why understanding someone's motivation matters. When there is understanding, meaningful trust can develop.

How we connect one to one, sometimes emotionally, sometimes through logic, sometimes through humor—our go-to GIF is the Millhouse frisbee toss—are all relevant. We believe these connections are as meaningful as discussions about return on investment, the lifetime value of customers, the cost of acquisition...Those pieces matter, yes, when it's time to make a purchasing decision for the Buying Committee.

But we connect human to human. Sometimes in ways that are hard to put into words or language. Sometimes the logic behind a decision is filled in later.

Everything that we teach within the operating system keeps human interaction in mind. That's why occasionally you'll see an email with bad grammar. Or a touchpoint to help just because we want to help. Or the emphasis on earning the right to someone's time. It's part of who we are.

## SALES IS A HUMAN ART

Sales is an art.

Automation and AI might make things easier, but relying solely on them and neglecting the fundamentals will actually hurt you in the long run.

It's crazy how every SEO expert, LinkedIn lead specialist, AI tool vendor, and outsourcing agency thinks I'm itching to buy their services.

And guess what?

Most of their messages cluttering my inbox look exactly the same.

I'm a huge fan of AI and automation tools. I use them every day. In fact, I'm diving deeper into video messaging with AI, and it's mind-blowing in relation to what can be done.

But the reality is that sticking to the basics is nonnegotiable.

Our prospects are drowning in noise, and cutting through that requires a personal touch.

Take a page from the brilliant Samantha McKenna: "Show them you know them."

This principle is more crucial now than ever.

Leverage LinkedIn Sales Navigator to build your lists and find triggers that warrant reaching out.

Morgan J Ingram is one of the masters at this, so follow his lead.

Here's the ultimate tip to drive more from your outreach.

Don't cut corners.

Put in the work if you want the results.

## PERSONAL RELATIONSHIPS

We continue to be reminded of the power of relationships.

It may seem like the deal that is about to close is the most important part of your funnel, but what if your relationship funnel is more important for the long term? We think it is.

| SALES FUNNEL | | | RELATIONSHIP FUNNEL |
|---|---|---|---|
| Short term ⧗ | Relationship type | ⏱ | Long term |
| Generating sales 💰 | Focuses on | 👥 | Building relationships |
| Fast ⏱ | Time to profit | ♡ | Nurturing relationships |
| Content & pressure tactics to generate sales 📢 | Strategies | 🏷 | Relational experience |
| Sales/ROI 💲 | Measurable metrics | 📈 | Relational performance |

Sometimes a deal doesn't go our way, but the power of those personal relationships remains if we stay true to giving value and doing the right thing.

So focus on building the right relationships.

Give without asking for anything in return.

## Meaningful Relationships

Working with some incredible folks at my favorite Australian football club (soccer), my son and I had the opportunity to experience a game from a different view and perspective—down on the pitch.

And we loved it.

Frequently, the goal in sales is the transaction. However, the most rewarding approach is to concentrate on assisting others rather than on the transaction.

If there is one change you can make to your sales approach that will help you differentiate in the sea of sameness...

It's focusing on building meaningful relationships.

## GIVE, GIVE, GIVE

A sales mindset that works every time:

Give value to others with no expectations.

Give your best ideas, thoughts, and recommendations.

For free.

Offer your services before the prospect pays you.

A couple of things that will happen:

1. They'll love you for it.
2. They'll hire you because of it.

Win-win.

It's a simple mindset shift:

- Stop thinking short-term.
- Stop thinking transactional.
- Stop trying to "close" everyone.

This mindset is long-term, relational, and builds trust.

It's profitable because it's focused on people, not just transactions.

Put simply:

*If you want to win, start by giving.*

# THE LAW OF RECIPROCITY

On a call with the JPAC region with LinkedIn, someone I helped was talking about their Sales Development Academy. She said, "We couldn't have done it without Lui."

Coming from someone who is ex-Google and who had achieved that within LinkedIn was special. And you know what? That relationship started with me saying, "I've done something for you; it'll help you with your new job."

Reciprocity is real. But don't do something because you're expecting something in return. Do it because you truly care about helping people.

Recently, one of our podcast listeners who stumbled upon us very early on and binged a few episodes became a client—five years later. That's a story that I'm happy to share. A number of times I was on the phone with him sharing tools and paths forward. I never knew if he would join up, but I did it because it was a genuine relationship.

If you focus on planting those seeds and contributing around you, that will build your brand, it'll build your network, and it *will* come back to you.

## Checkpoint 10:
## An Automation Audit

*Just as there are checkpoints in a sales and buying journey, there will be checkpoints through this book to test your learning and application: learning without application is simply entertainment.*

### The Art of Selling with a System

*AI cannot outsell humans...yet.*

*This checkpoint is a chance to review all the tools we use daily. How much time are we spending with them? What do they help us do? Where are they missing? Are we using too many? Not enough? Make a list: Name of tool, For, Advantage, Disadvantage. What did you learn from this? Are there tools to leave out? Or do you need to invest in one or two more? What window of time will you give yourself to onboard or integrate that tool?*

## SOUND BYTE SUMMARY

— Prospecting every day maintains the human connection. It also makes sure that the pipeline won't suffer in two to three months.

— Even if you're using automation, look for ways to add human touches into each stage of the sales process.

— Give away your ideas and your services for free without thinking of return.

> To get access to all of the templates, frameworks, tools, and podcast episodes referenced in this book, visit this link: **growthforum.io/bonuses**

## NEXT UP

Let's get you over the finish line!

# Conclusion:

# THE FINISH LINE

There's no point overthinking it. Sales is simple. It's about helping others. Learn what they need and help them reach a great outcome by facilitating every step of the buying journey.

The sales operating system that you've built helps you keep it simple and focused on the people.

A flood of qualified leads is your potential. If you follow the steps, if you are consistent, if you are fueled by a winning mindset, then it's within reach.

Paul J. Meyer, who Lui listened to on repeat driving to morning gym sessions, talked about how to learn: (1) tell me, (2) show me, (3) let me, (4) correct me.

Do that enough times with what you've learned in this book and you are on your way not only to developing a solid sales operating system, but to performing at your own top level as the operator of that system.

Use the engine you've built for repeatable results, but never stop learning. Again, it's your mindset that maintains the slight edge in the areas that matter, no matter what changes in the marketplace, economy, or the level of technology.

We've touched on a lot in this book, so keep it on your desk or nightstand for reference.

By chapter, here's what you've learned:

1. Starting with *a growth mindset* leads to an always-learning attitude, which leads to embracing the sales first principles, which puts one on the road to becoming a true sales professional.

2. Decide *who your best customer could be (ICP)*, then draw them in detail (Buyer Persona).

3. *Map out every stage of your sales process* in light of the buying journey.

4. *Put buyers first*, assessing everything from their position to properly enable them tangibly and psychologically.

5. How sellers are initially engaged is crucial to *the first conversation, where value must be given.*

6. *Earning the right through value-driven communication* by phone, email, text message, video, and other technological methods yet to go mainstream.

7. Effectively nurture deals with a focus on developing and

*validating the business case,* starting with the commercial return on investment.

8. Approach the members of the Buying Committee at the right time with *the right information tailored to them* and their individual desires, concerns, and motivations.

9. *Continue providing value all the way through to deal closing* by handling objections well and let the business case drive that decision.

10. While tech will help, *the human connection trumps* because people prefer to buy from and enjoy buying from people they trust.

We're hopeful that you will embrace the infinite game that is sales with the motivation to help people. That means doing free work sometimes because it is the right thing to do, with no other thought of gain. Much more than that, it means living up to the standard that you set for yourself, because you can be your best coach through self-coaching.

But if you still want a sounding board—maybe even to discuss how to become a great self-coach—get a free sales clarity call with us: https://www.growthforum.io/apply

Starting this structured, designed learning space and then building momentum was possible because the traditional education system has let B2B companies down, with a complete lack of formal teaching in sales and go-to-market. That means 100+ million people across the planet are learning on the job, and every person responsible for revenue is at constant risk of missing their targets, and often do.

Of course, it doesn't have to be that way—we saw that problem, and instead of choosing to think small, we are trying to be part of the solution.

Now, before we sign off: remember, there are a lot of good ideas that have yet to be implemented across the world, and good salespeople can be the facilitators of those beneficial, even game-changing ideas.

Seeing that bigger picture will help to put yourself in the context of an even larger infinite game, which is improving the lives of those around you, whether they be family members, friends, neighbors, or complete strangers, on the road to a dynamic world with peaceful prosperity for all.

There's just one more thing…

Belief. It's the foundation of all dreams. Growth Forum was built because we believe in the people who rise every day, striving to create something extraordinary. Sales is the most rewarding job in the world, but it's also one of the toughest. What works today may not work tomorrow. Why? Because we're not just dealing with products; we're dealing with people and emotions.

A wise mentor once told me, "Everyone needs something to believe in, someone to believe in, and someone who believes in them." This simple truth has stuck with me throughout my career.

At Growth Forum, we believe in you, the ones getting up, putting in the work, and pushing forward. Now, with the tools, knowledge, and support we provide, you're equipped to reach that next level of success.

Remember, there are no barriers to what you can achieve. The opportunities are endless because we live in a world of abundance, where anything is possible. All you have to do is take action.

# YOUR VOICE MATTERS

If this book has sparked a new way of thinking, given you a tool you've implemented, or even just challenged you to reflect on your sales process, we have a small favor to ask. Your insights and experiences are invaluable—not just to us, but to others searching for a sales operating system that truly works.

A quick review, whether online or shared with a peer, helps amplify the reach of these ideas. It ensures this system finds its way to those who need it most. Plus, your feedback helps us grow and refine this work for future readers.

Write your review over at: **growthforum.io/review**

Thank you for taking this journey with us.

Now, let's share the impact and keep building!

# STEP BY STEP PLAYBOOK TO CLOSING AN EIGHT-FIGURE DEAL

# Laying out the significant steps in a real deal, the first eight-figure deal of Luigi's career, through an interview with the champion of the Buying Committee

Here's a recent conversation between Luigi and Marcus, reflecting on when they worked together on the News Corp deal in 2011 and 2012. Notice each of the steps that were taken through the buying and selling journey.

**Luigi:** When we started working together on that transformation, what was your role?

**Marcus:** Thanks, Luigi. When we first started working together, I was in a national production role, probably back in 2011, 2012. And I had been running the Sydney Print Center, and I'd moved into running all the print centers around the country. And that was looking after, I think at that time there would have been nine print centers, or maybe 10, with close to 1,200 or 1,300 people.

**Luigi:** At the time you took over, what specific challenge prompted you to begin looking at vendors to help with that transformation initiative that you led?

**Marcus:** The role was based on the premise of change. Newspapers needed to change. I mean, it's no secret that volumes have been declining for quite some time now. And the old model of "get it out the door and get it on the lawn" was no longer relevant. So we had to be more efficient. And one of the things we spoke about was there's a runway for newspapers.

And we had to make that as efficient as possible. So it meant really changing the way the entire workforce changed and changing the way our leaders led. And that was a task I needed support with.

Luigi: What was the criteria you had in your mind when you were evaluating vendors?

Marcus: I'd previously done a little bit of work with one vendor in Sydney when I was running the Sydney Print Centre, LMA. And that was really taking all the leaders through the Challenger Leadership Program. The reason I picked that one: it was a nine-month program, so you had to earn your stripes. It wasn't just a week in a classroom and then you're on your own and good luck. This was nine months of support. So the people going through it felt like they were going through torture at times because they hadn't done that much studying for quite a while. But it made them realize they'd earned it when they got it. And it really changed people's lives.

So when I got the national role, I wanted to do something similar for all the leaders across the country, to give them the skills. (A) To be able to leave. So they didn't feel like they were stuck to the organization. They had some transferable skills that they could take elsewhere. So they had choice. But also, (B) to have a whole lot of people that were thinking the way I wanted to think and let them change the organization.

Luigi: At what point, when you first started engaging with me, at what point did the relationship shift from salesperson or vendor to trusted advisor, if you can remember?

**Marcus:** Yeah, I might step back a step before that, Luigi. I think we had our first meeting at Port Melbourne, which I think for you wasn't a very good meeting. You came in selling me something I didn't want. I wanted the leadership program first to get the leaders on board because I had trouble with all of those leaders. Then I wanted to come through with competitive manufacturing or some level of training for all the staff. And that first meeting you brought along a chap who was really pushing heavy on the training at your frontline staff first and this is what we can do.

So where it worked is I think you took the learning from not getting the message right in the first meeting. You went away and did your work and really understood my business a lot better and what I was trying to achieve and came back with a plan of what I wanted. So the second meeting was a lot better in terms of understanding what it was that I wanted and providing a map of that.

Then the amount of time you invested in understanding my business, like even though you'd done the work for that second meeting, you kept going harder to try and understand more of what it was that I needed and then started offering up what I needed. And that very first one I think you brought in what you *thought* I needed. A hell lot of work went on, and that just built the trust that this guy's actually invested in what I'm trying to achieve.

**Luigi:** When that occurred, when I started to spend time on your print floor, I think it was at one, two, three o'clock in the morning. Yeah. And I started to share some of that insight with you. Did that impact your perspective on what the strategy needed to be in order to achieve your goal?

**Marcus:** I don't think it did. Because I think you spent time trying to understand what it was I wanted. So it was very aligned. Look, it might have been a deviation or iteration, but it wasn't a wholesale shift of where I was trying to take things. You definitely spent time with the guys on the floor—who weren't an easy mob, by the way—understanding what it was that was blocking them. And so I think you helped facilitate how to get that group in line with the vision.

But I don't think the vision changed. The vision was always very much there. But what you brought was getting in, understanding what it was I was trying to achieve, where I was at, and what tools, at that time was LMA or Think Perform, could bring to help support it.

**Luigi:** And from your experiences with other people that have sold you things or that you've purchased from, how did the interaction with me differ from others that you've purchased from in the past?

**Marcus:** You listened.

I mean, stepping back to that first meeting, I think my feedback to you was fairly blunt. I don't shy away from giving the honest truth. And you listened and went away and tweaked. We've had other people come through in other fields, not the training realm, and they thought they've known the answers. Whether they need to modify for my environment or not, but you gotta listen. And if you don't listen, you don't get the engagement, you don't get the trust.

So I think the bit that worked for you and the reason we engaged you across such 1,200 people and training them on a two-year program was because you listened at the outset and you helped develop a program I needed.

**Luigi:** Yeah, fantastic. If we think about the amount of people and stakeholders, when we started to build the business case, can you just walk through what were some of the internal roadblocks that you encountered and did the relationship with me help support you?

Working through those roadblocks and for example, another GM, the print secretary...can you just walk us through?

**Marcus:** Finance as well, return on investment. There were so many angles. I mean, it's not unusual for a project this size to have a lot of humps to get over.

When you're investing in people, when you're doing any investment, what's the return? What are you going to get out of it? And to have the...I guess the nonquantitative benefits, it's hard for the finance guys to get their head around that that's worth the investment. So I had to have the nonquantitative but also the very quantitative. And I think some of the tools that your team was able to bring was, yeah, he's demonstrating some of the numbers that are gonna be pulled out. So there was a portal that was built to say, "Hey, these are the actual dollars that you're gonna save." So the promise that we're gonna be able to support the finance guys in an ROI was pretty important.

Not all my peers agreed that this is the right path to take. Just want to get on and do it and tell people what to do. I'm not a strong believer in the direction approach. I think you've got to engage as you go. And I think one of things we spoke about earlier on, and LMA did a good job in developing the model, and remember the inverted pyramid? Where the leaders are there to support the frontline workforce.

That was pretty controversial for a lot of people in my business that actually like to tell people what to do, I suppose, to support the front line. I had to navigate. And your model helps navigate that. It put my mind in a clear picture on a page to spread that vision.

**Luigi:** I guess that was part of the transformation too, right? Like we weren't just enabling the leaders and the staff, we were *shifting* the way in which the business was leading, right? It was very top heavy. And so I think that was a big part of it, which people...

**Marcus:** And it was saying to them, it was taking people out of their comfort zone. The people that led forever in one way and telling them that that was not the way of the future, if there was going to be a good future, was quite confronting. Then in my business, the whole time I've been doing it, we've been having redundancies as the business has shrunk. We've had to shed people.

So the National Secretary of the AMWU, her first concern was this was just going to be another tool for selecting people to go out the door. So I had to convince her that's not what it was. And fortunately, I've developed a good relationship with her over the years. And there was a certain amount of trust there. It was work to talk to her. And then, I mean, the hard work you had to do was go and talk to the staff on the floor to convince them of what it was and what it wasn't.

Luigi: Yeah, and if I recall, we didn't just have the internal executive team that we had to get across the line. We had to get the printing division, the external stakeholders, and then we had to be on the floor. So we probably engaged with what, a few hundred people as part of that sales process?

Marcus: And even though we've got the head of the union on board, it didn't necessarily mean that the heads of the union at print centers were on board. Whilst there's alignment, there's misalignment, or when the doors close, they don't necessarily bind to the message that the secretary was delivering. So yeah, there were a lot of conversations, as you said, at two in the morning.

Luigi: And just moving to that business case, right? You mentioned the financial component and showing the finance guy what the return on investment is, but from a business case perspective, did we cocreate that business case or was it you created it or was it a partnership and when we created it?

Marcus: It was a 100% joint effort. I mean, we had to do it for (1) internal and (2) we were seeking funding. I can't remember the body, we were seeking funding from the time.

Luigi: Think we got the largest grant of its kind for the manufacturing sector.

**Marcus:** Yeah, so that when I say we worked on it together, I think I might have done 10%. You might have turned it 90%. And look, there was the one that was internal. I tweaked it for internal language, which, you know, that's kind of my gig to make it work internally. But the one that was for external use was probably more than 90% your language because you knew how it had to fit to get the external funding. So yeah, it was very much a joint role.

**Luigi:** Would love to pick your brain here, right? So let's talk about the business case. You've purchased sites, you've purchased multimillion-dollar equipment for your plants. What are the top three things that every one of your internal business cases needs to showcase?

**Marcus:** Number one is return on investment. "What's it going to cost?" is the first thing. So where's your capital coming from? And that's an issue for every company. And we had a good balance sheet, have a good balance sheet. So it wasn't a question of that, but it was prioritizing the money.

So an organization is going through a digital transformation. You're arguing against people that want to have a new app, a new website, something that's in line with the future strategy as opposed to someone who was competing for old strategy. So share of capital was a big thing. But then it was return on investment. So what are we going to get back? And how is that stacking up against the others? And three, is it on strategy?

**Luigi:** And is there a risk component in there as well that you sort of think about like the risk of, you know, not working or working out? Does that become a conversation that happens?

**Marcus:** There's always a risk element to them all. So that's with all major projects. We've built new print centers, we close print centers, we amalgamate print centers, and you always look at what can go wrong. And then we run one risk workshop over a whole raft of financial, reputational risk, safety risk, the whole gamut we go through. So yeah, there's a risk profile.

**Luigi:** So we've got the business case. Now let's talk about the proposal. So you've had a lot of proposals put on your desk. When you pick up a proposal, it doesn't matter if it's five pages or a hundred pages, what part of it do you actually read?

**Marcus:** I won't get past the first page if it's not engaging with what I want. If the email leading into it, like if it's a cold call, that's hard. The email's got to pique the interest. But if it's something I've asked for, pretty quickly on the first page, I can tell whether it's on song or not. And if it's not on song, if it's way off, then someone hasn't done their work.

And if it's a bit off, then you'll call them and say, "Hey, I think you missed this." But if it's on song, then you'll read through it. But you know pretty quickly if someone's listened to the brief or not.

**Luigi:** So that first page is critical, really.

**Marcus:** 100%. I mean, it's said far too often about being busy people, but, you know, when you're looking after a large team, you have multiple divisions, you're growing a business. And I was trying to grow a business that was not doing any external printing to in excess of a $50 million business. And that there was a lot I was doing. If someone couldn't hit the brief on the first page and take the time to get it right early on, then it's kind of not respecting what I've put out there and what I'm looking for.

Luigi: Now I've got two final questions for you Marcus. So there was a point in our relationship, and I was 28, 29 years of age in 2011.

There was a moment that you brought me into a meeting where there was the CEO, the CFO, and there was your immediate report. At that point, how did you view me at that time, coming into a significant internal meeting?

Marcus: I think by that stage, you'd spend a lot of time in the business. So we had built the business plan. You'd spend a lot of time understanding what was going on. I mean, outside of that, I mean, you and I had started running together around Melbourne. So we developed a personal trust as well as the business trust. So there was more to it than just the business relationship where you'd spend the time getting to know what I wanted. You'd actually spend the time getting to know me.

At the time we had that senior meeting, a lot of the work had been done. So internally I'd laid the foundations with all those people. Because of the investment we were making, they wanted to meet the person who was going to be taking the money.

But knowing how you presented, knowing how you've done the work, I wouldn't have invited that meeting if you didn't know my business, you didn't know what it was about, because it just would have been a failure. But you're able to talk about the business, you're able to talk about what it was I was trying to achieve and how you're going to deliver it. So I think in the end, it was actually a pretty quick meeting. Reading the room that was there, they were pretty quickly on board that you'd done the work. If I wasn't in a position where I was comfortable that you would be singing from the same hymn sheet as me, you wouldn't have been in that meeting. But we spent time together, and you knew what it was, and I trust you to follow this group.

**Luigi:** Yeah. It's funny. My kids still remember those nights where I would drive to the print center, the Herald Sun print center in Melbourne. They'd say, "Dad's going again." They remember me working night shift. I never worked night shift. And just the last question, Marcus, the very last question.

**Marcus:** Sorry, before that. With manufacturing, night shift is the forgotten shift in every business. And most manufacturers operate on day shift. They only flow into night shift if their machine capacity is so much they can't get enough done on days. And I heard that when I was at Colgate, they had one shift with the majority on day shift. At News, because it's newspaper, you're all on night shift.

Everyone says they care. No one visits night shift because it's such an ugly shift to go to. And the fact that you visited night shift, got to know the night shift people, got to understand our business on the back shift, showed you were interested in what the business was doing.

And it's a real telltale sign. We get new people coming into the business. And I'll say to them, the best time to see it is to go to a print center on a Friday night. It's when it's its busiest, and you'll see everything in operation, see all the people.

But people want to go and have a beer with their mates on a Friday night. They don't want to go to a print center. And so it is the best test of how invested someone is if they go in on a Friday night, and you went in.

**Luigi:** We went in nine different print centers across every state and territory.

And just the last question. Can you recall that, that famous day on October 13th in, what was it? 2012 or 13? What happened at Chicago Marathon?

**Marcus:** You did the moonwalk to Michael Jackson back to front as you were running along. Unfortunately, it was just as you went past me. So I was able to see it, which is a sight I can't get out of my memory. Let's bring on Seoul. But you're a much younger man than me. But what was your PB by the way?

**Luigi:** 3:23.

**Marcus:** Okay, so when you get under 3:06 and you qualify for Boston, give me a buzz.

**Luigi:** All right, all right. I'm gonna try very hard for Seoul. But Marcus, thank you, man. This has been great.

# ABOUT THE AUTHORS

**DAVID FASTUCA** | Meet David, a powerhouse in revenue growth. During his time at Locomote.com, he generated an impressive $150 million sales pipeline in less than 18 months—even amid COVID-19—by applying the same system you'll learn about in this book. As a successful exited founder (with over $30 million in exits), his approach turns obstacles into opportunities, helping businesses thrive in any economic climate. His CMO background adds a unique depth to the training offered at Growth Forum.

**LUIGI PRESTINENZI** | Meet Luigi, a master in sales who has perfected the art and science of closing deals from $5,000 to $100 million. His strategy goes beyond simple transactions, transforming each deal into a memorable experience and building meaningful, lasting connections. Luigi has trained founders and sales teams from some of the most successful B2B brands, bringing invaluable insights into creating predictable, scalable sales processes.

www.ingramcontent.com/pod-product-compliance
Lightning Source LLC
Chambersburg PA
CBHW040752220326
41597CB00029BA/4739